NINE WOMEN IN THE BIBLE WHO CAN
HELP YOU LIVE YOUR LIFE BOLDLY

What Will They Think?

GRACE VALENTINE

W PUBLISHING GROUP

AN IMPRINT OF THOMAS NELSON

ISBN 978-0-7852-9306-4 (audiobook)
ISBN 978-0-7852-9305-7 (eBook)
ISBN 978-0-7852-9304-0 (TP)

Library of Congress Cataloging-in-Publication Data

Library of Congress Control Number: 2022002732

Printed in the United States of America

22 23 24 25 26 LSC 10 9 8 7 6 5 4 3 2 1

To Debbie Wickwire: Thank you for believing in twenty-year-old me. I was so sad you retired but happy that this book could be one of our last projects together. I am better for knowing you. I pray that one day I can help raise up more women in their calling in the way you raised me. Thank you for being bold and teaching me to be bold. You will always be my book mom and a cheerleader in my life!

And to the women in the Bible whom I hope to meet in heaven one day: Thank you for reminding me that women were never afterthoughts for God. Thank you for teaching me to be bold. I pray to have your strength.

Contents

PART 4: WHAT WILL THEY THINK IF I OBEY GOD?

PART 5: WHAT WILL THEY THINK IF I'M AN OUTCAST?

PART 6: WHAT WILL THEY THINK IF MY LIFE IS TRANSFORMED?

PART 7: WHAT WILL THEY THINK IF I'M ORDINARY?

INTRODUCTION

BOOK INTRODUCTIONS ARE WEIRD, ESPECIALLY WHEN you're the one writing them. There is so much I want to say, but I don't want to scare you off. I want you to be intrigued. I want you to be reading the introduction while drinking your coffee and thinking, *Yep! This is going to be a good one. I can feel it.*

Introductions feel weird because I'm worried what you will think about me. And there are a lot of things I want to result from this two-thousand-word introduction:

- I want to convince you that this book is relatable.
- I want to convince you that I'm not a weird or boring Christian. I want you to think I'm a fun girl who would watch your favorite reality TV show with you.
- I want you to flip to the back of the book, see the picture of me, and think it looks good. I know it's silly, but I got my roots touched up before I took that shot, so I want you to think I'm decently cute.
- I want you to believe that Scripture can help you work through the problem you are struggling with.
- Oh, and I really want you to like me. I can't help but wonder, *What will she think about me after she reads this introduction?*

I hate to admit that last part. I wish I could say I was this chill girl who never cared about what you, a stranger I may never meet, thought about me. But the truth is I'm sitting here typing worried about whether you will like me or truly understand that I have your back. I really want you to think, *Dang, I would love to hang out with that girl and just talk about life.* And I wish I could say that whenever someone talks about me behind my back, I pray for reconciliation and shrug it off. But I'm not a "shrug it off" type of girl. I'm more of an "obsess over every word someone says and overanalyze my actions to the point where it makes me socially awkward" type of girl.

I get anxious around people I want to impress, even strangers. I get in my head and come up with lies about how I think others perceive me. Unfortunately, this anxiety and desire to be liked has often stopped me from being bold.

Anyone else feel like this?

What will they think? is a question that has stopped me from doing what I feel called to do more times than I can count. Let me start by saying that the word *called* can be overused and confusing. You may be thinking, *Great, another Christian writer is talking about knowing that God has called her to do something when I don't know if I even picked the right major.*

It can be confusing to know what you're called to do. Being called isn't necessarily hearing a deep voice yell at you or getting the chills, and there's rarely a burning bush. Being called is feeling a tug on your heart to do something that would glorify God and align with Scripture. It's that prompting to text an old friend and ask how she is doing. It's that urge you feel to lead a Bible study for high schoolers. It's that desire to make a difference in your hometown or the nudge you feel to ask someone if they need a helping hand. We have all been called by God to do something, and you, too, might feel a calling on your heart right now. But I think we can all admit that we have neglected a call before because we were too busy thinking, *What will they think?*

One thing I've learned is that being bold is a verb, not a destination. You can't just bibbidi-bobbidi-boo yourself into being bold; you must choose boldness daily and learn how to stop caring about what others will think of you. Even as the author of this book, I have to remind myself not to care what you will think about me as you read it. I care about your struggles and your burdens, and I care for your heart and your purpose, so I constantly have to remind myself to focus on all those things instead of wasting my energy worrying about whether you think I'm cool.

When I wrote my first book, there was one chapter I felt nudged to redo before it was published. Originally, I cared too much about what my mom and grandma would think when they read a specific personal story, but I finally realized the book wasn't for them. So after months of ignoring the nudge, I emailed my amazing publisher at the last minute, and they let me change it to include that personal story. How sad would it have been if I had missed out on what God was saying to me because I was worried about my grandma knowing I made mistakes? How sad would it be for you to miss out on a career, service opportunity, relationship, conversation, or God's best for you because you were too worried about what people might think?

If you picked up this book, you, too, probably want your life to be about more than being liked. Perhaps you want to do big things that make a difference in your community or even our world. It's okay if you and I are not the picture-perfect "cool girls." The women in the Bible weren't cool and put together either. They were regular women like you and me who chose to be bold.

I think the world today defines boldness differently than Scripture. Nowadays when people speak their minds, the world calls this bold. We aren't called to speak our minds. We are called to speak the Spirit. True boldness requires courage, self-control, humility, and wisdom. Boldness doesn't require perfection, just a perfect God working out the details for His good and our good. I love the women in the Bible because I believe they each uniquely displayed boldness. Sometimes they spoke their faith, and sometimes they allowed their gentleness and love to be louder than their opinions. Sometimes their boldness was shown through a position they were given, other times through humble arms that were ready to love a neighbor. Boldness isn't exclusive to the loud personalities. It is given by the Holy Spirit and is available to all of us. When we see how these biblical women decided to be bold in their trust, position, faith, and thankfulness, we can begin to understand how beautiful boldness can be in our own lives.

So as I write this book, let me remind you how uncool I am, and let me remind myself that my purpose is to live out my calling boldly, not to be liked. I didn't make the cheer team in middle school (twice), I am terrible at dating at the age of twenty-five, and like many girls my age, I'm on dating apps (it's scary out there, folks). I love the idea of planning a party but then freak out and cancel out of fear no one will show up. I was furloughed from my main source of income during COVID-19, and it was hard. I had just bought a house, so I didn't get an actual couch for months. I love Jesus, but I went a little crazy in college. I once threw up hungover in a Chick-fil-A drive-through at eleven o'clock in the morning. So if you think I'm a hot mess, not the typical "cool girl" Christian author, that's okay. I feel called to write this book for girls like me who have an unhealthy obsession with what others think—because that causes them to miss out on their true purpose. If you feel like you're ready to live life boldly and stop caring about what others think, then this book is for you. From one hot mess and former people pleaser to another, *let's do this*.

Even though I still struggle with caring about what others will think of me, I have gotten a lot better at choosing boldness rather than focusing on pleasing others. In my early twenties I felt called to live differently but was worried others would think I was trying too hard. People thinking I was trying to do something new and risking my normal? Ugh, how embarrassing! Except it's not embarrassing. We've all been there, worried that others will gossip about our efforts to step into something crazy. After college I wanted to walk in boldness but always waited for others' permission. Then after becoming a retired party girl, I discovered that even those in the Christian community care too much about what others think. I realized that many Christian women were like me and just wanted to make others happy. My frustration with the worldly desire to please came from the belief that my role as a woman was to be pretty, to smile, and to be likeable. But I lost my ability to be bold through this outlook, and I realized that no matter how hard I tried to be likeable, there was always someone who didn't like me. Shocking, right?

So I opened my Bible. For the longest time I had thought the Bible was just stories about men walking with Jesus. I thought the Bible taught women to be quiet, polite sidekicks. Some Christians led me to believe this, and maybe you've been led to believe this too. One day, I got a message that said, "I just hate that the Bible hates women." I remember my jaw dropping. *Hate*? What a strong word. But here's the truth: if you believe the lie that women are afterthoughts in Scripture, you'll likely also believe the lie that God hates women.

At first I thought this message was dramatic, but then I

realized I was on the path to believing this also. And yet I didn't think my God truly felt this way, so I read Scripture and looked for the women. Here is what I found:

Jesus listens to women.

Jesus calls women to be on His team.

Jesus doesn't ask for "perfect" women; He calls for bold women.

Jesus hears our frustrations.

Jesus listens to our tired and restless hearts.

Jesus calls us to be kind and loving, not likeable.

Jesus wants us to stop trying to meet everyone's expectations.

Women were never afterthoughts. In fact, the Bible was written during a time when the culture made women even more of an afterthought than they are now. But women were included in Scripture and placed there by our God so you and I could have examples of bold women. We aren't perfect, we may get nervous, and we may try to manipulate our situations like some women in the Bible did, but we aren't merely sidekicks. Women in the Bible were offered moments of boldness and given lessons to learn, and their stories are woven into Scripture.

If you know me personally, you know I have always advocated for women's empowerment. I am all for breaking glass ceilings. I used to think that if I wanted to take my faith seriously, I would have to discard my desire for women to feel empowered. I thought I couldn't break glass ceilings if I was following Christ. But we can't have true women empowerment without first acknowledging the most powerful being in this world. If we don't know our Creator, how can we know why we were created? If I have a daughter someday, I want her to wait on the Lord but not wait to live life boldly in Christ's name. I want her to see in Scripture that Jesus listened to women and that Jesus listens to her. I want her to realize that her purpose is not to be liked but to be bold.

We need to stop being afraid of others not liking us. We were not created to please others. Our focus needs to be on living for God.

In this book I want us to examine nine women in the Bible and notice these four things about each of them:

- God heard her.
- She wasn't perfect; she just knew her perfect God.
- God used her.
- She focused on her purpose, not on how others viewed her.

I want you to forget the lie that Jesus wants quiet and one-dimensional women on His team. Throughout this book, you will see that you can be bold and gentle, purposeful and true to your personality, humble and confident, a little messy yet expectant, and even misunderstood and forgiven. Jesus listens to women, but to walk in purpose, we must listen to Him.

I want us to learn from these women in the Bible. But let me be clear: they weren't perfect. They did some great things, but they weren't the dream team. Thankfully, the beautiful thing is that our God isn't looking for perfection. He isn't looking to use only the ones with the best stats and the most experience. He is looking for you. Yes, you. We serve a God who wants to use us right where we are. He knows that through faith and boldness we can do great things. When we know who our big God is, we can do big things. These big things aren't necessarily going to make us likeable, give us financial success, or win us worldly affirmation, but they will give us something better: God. His peace and courage will enable us to walk boldly in His purpose for us.

God wants you to be bold, starting now.

You are loved and wanted, and God wants you on His team. You have a calling and a purpose. Life is about something more important than being liked. Life is about being His and walking in the purpose He gives you. If you're struggling to embrace this truth, I encourage you to focus on Scripture and ask God how He can use you where you are. And now, let's start this journey together.

PART 1

What Will They Think If I Speak Up?

For if you remain silent at this time, relief and deliverance for the Jews will arise from another place, but you and your father's family will perish. And who knows but that you have come to your royal position for such a time as this?

ESTHER 4:14

CHAPTER 1

Learn from Esther

there was unde age drinking going on before the event, so my

IN 2016 I WAS A NEW SORORITY GIRL WHO WANTED TO be cool. I finally had been asked out to a "cool" fraternity semi-formal. I found a long-sleeved, tight, black minidress to impress the cute guy who'd asked me. As most college students know, there was underage drinking going on before the event, so my date asked me, "What kind of alcohol do you like?"

Even though I had only dabbled with underage drinking and tried weird punches at frat houses and occasionally other basic drinks, for some reason I said, "Whiskey!"

His eyes lit up.

Drinking underage is illegal, and it's also a sin, just like lying. And lying is exactly what my fruit-punch mixxy, margarita-loving, basic-girl self was doing when I said I loved whiskey. I threw up at that semiformal after attempting one shot. (I'll add here that anyone who claims underage drinking is fun is wrong.)

You've probably realized that I said I was a whiskey girl because I wanted to be cool. I wanted to be the chill girl who was one of the boys, like the main character in a rom-com movie, because that's what I thought boys wanted. But I'm not a whiskey girl, I'm not a cool girl, and I'm not one of the boys.

Now I can look back at myself pretending to like whiskey and chuckle. It is sad, sinful, and shameful that I thought if I were a whiskey girl, some frat boy would like me more. It is pitiful that I thought I needed to drink in order to have confidence or for him to like me.

Unfortunately, this wasn't the only time I altered myself to be who I thought someone wanted me to be. I once dated a guy who didn't like my physical boundaries, and I felt I needed to change this to please him. I struggled with my relationships with family members because I assumed they didn't like me, and I thought I had to be a different type of person to gain their respect. I had friends I feared would gossip about me, so I hid my personality, emotions, and struggles in hopes they would like me.

I have also been silent on issues important to me because I was scared of what others would think of me. *Will they think I'm not smart enough to speak on this? Will they cancel me if I don't say things perfectly or if they disagree? Is it better to not try at all? Will they think I'm trying too hard or not see my intentions? Will I annoy someone or make them uncomfortable by speaking up? What if I simply do something that makes me not likeable? Isn't my purpose to be liked?*

We've all been there. But if there is anything we can learn from Esther, it is that we were not called to be who others want us to be. We don't have to conform to the roles others wish we would play. We are in the roles God has prepared us for, and we don't have to fit in someone else's box. We can be bold and speak up, and when we do, we will find more purpose than we would by being silent.

In this chapter we'll see how Esther did not conform to who others wanted her to be. Life was out of her control in a lot of ways. She didn't have a say in who she married, where she lived, her career, or her education, but she did have control over her words. She spoke up and lived out her calling.

In the book that bears her name, we quickly learn that Esther was placed in a kind of beauty pageant for Xerxes, the king of Persia, to find a new wife. Her life wasn't easy; she had lost her parents, so her older cousin became her father figure and guardian. This cousin, Mordecai, had been carried into exile from Jerusalem and worked in the Persian government. Their lives were hard and humble. When Esther joined the other beautiful women brought to the king's competition at the palace, Mordecai instructed her not to share her Jewish nationality and family background (Est. 2:10).

Was this basically like a season of *The Bachelor*? I don't know. I'm sure if they had reality TV back then, everyone would have been tuning in to see this play out. Would my best friends and I be watching "The King's Season" waiting to see the drama play out on his "journey"? But Esther didn't have a choice about being there. No one happened to "submit her application." She was just chosen from a poor, small community. Ultimately, Esther was chosen by the king to be his wife. It is hard to know whether she wanted this or not. We don't know what her thoughts leading up to the pageant were. We do know she underwent extensive beauty treatments and won the favor of those around her (Est. 2:12–15).

After also winning the favor of the king, Esther's life changed overnight. As she transitioned to life at the palace, she stayed close to her cousin, Mordecai. At one point Mordecai informed Esther that he had overheard two guards conspiring to kill the king. Esther immediately alerted the king. Xerxes was very grateful to both Esther and Mordecai after hearing about the threat to his life.

Things seem to be going favorably for Esther, until we encounter a man named Haman. Mordecai was a Jewish man of integrity, and when Haman, the king's second-in-command, ordered all the king's servants to bow to him, Mordecai remained faithful to God and refused. This upset Haman so much that he conspired to convince Xerxes to sign a decree issuing all Jews in his kingdom to be killed. When Mordecai heard this, he tore his clothes in mourning and sat outside the king's gate in sackcloth and ashes (Est. 4:1–3). When Esther was informed about Mordecai, she went to see him and learned of Haman's evil plot. Mordecai advised her, "For if you remain silent at this time, relief and deliverance for the Jews will arise from another place, but you and your father's family will perish. And who knows but that you have come to your royal position for such a time as this?" (Est. 4:14).

With Mordecai's words in mind, Esther bravely entered the king's court without invitation, which could have gotten her killed. By the grace of God, King Xerxes heard her request and Haman's plot was revealed and thwarted. Because Esther spoke up and stood firm in her faith, she ended up saving her people. Haman was executed for his plot to destroy the Jews, which included the queen herself, and today a Jewish holiday honors Esther, whose boldness led to her saving the Jewish people.

I think we can all agree that declaring your faith in the midst of a decree killing fellow believers is not the same as saying "I like whiskey" to a frat boy to sound cool. But the truth is, in my younger twenties I lied about many parts of me. I lied about hobbies I had because they sounded weird. I was hesitant to go to church out of fear that people would be confused as to why the partying sorority girl would even think she belonged at church. I pretended to be confident and sassy when I was really the most insecure I had ever been. I pretended I enjoyed drinking, when really I regretted every night I drank, especially when waking up with fear after blacking out.

I played pretend. I pretended to be anyone but my true self. But this game isn't fun, because when you're projecting lies about yourself, how can truth ever enter your heart? If you aren't confident even in the little things about yourself, how can you find confidence in the reason you were created? If you can't speak up in a Monday morning meeting, how can you speak up for your morals?

I want you to think of all the times you chose fitting in over walking in boldness.

I want you to think of all the times you tried to save face and not save others.

I want you to think of all the times you were worried about the response, so you avoided responding with truth.

We've all done this.

But Esther didn't hide the part of her that could have caused her to be killed. She chose boldness and stood up for her people. She chose God's best for her purpose, though it wasn't safe— but it was her. She risked not being liked, not being wanted, not being alive to stand for truth. Even though Esther could have died simply by approaching the king, she spoke up. She had no control over who she married. She was forced to be as perfect as possible before being presented to the king. She lived in a time when women didn't have education or many rights. But she still spoke up. She still followed what she was called to do.

I think our society has intentionally tried to change a woman's purpose. It teaches women that we are made to please and not meant to step up.

I remember when I was seventeen, I struggled with body image. I spent many days unhealthily trying to shiver away another pound. I thought my purpose was to please others and be as tiny as I could be. I also thought my voice needed to be small. Sadly, the world seems to be telling women that their bodies, voices, and purposes need to be small in order for them to be liked. I hid my emotions and missed out on opportunities to spread the gospel because I didn't want to step on anyone's toes or I worried that it wasn't my place.

Not only does society tell women to be small, but recently I've noticed it's telling girls to be their own heroes. We promote independence to the point where it becomes unhealthy, making it difficult for women to trust community, friends, and especially God. We say we want to be "girl bosses," but the truth is we just want to write our own stories. But we don't hold the pen, and we aren't the authors, so when life doesn't go our way, we feel defeated; we feel unlikeable and incapable of being bold.

My prayer for you and me is that we will remember we are not sidekicks waiting for the approval of others, or, worse, waiting for someone to like us. We are all given the opportunity that Esther was given—to live out God's best and God's purpose for us. But to do this we have to risk not being liked.

Contrary to what the world says, we are not heroes in charge of our own stories. We are not meant to save the day, but we are called to be bold and point to the One who can save the hearts of everyone.

I often wonder if Esther, a poor girl who was part of a persecuted religion, raised by her cousin and picked to be the wife of the king, ever thought, *Why me? Why am I queen? Why am I in this palace as a Jewish girl?*

You may be thinking *Why?* as well. Why are you at this job, in this town, at this college? Why do you know this friend? Perhaps, like Esther, you grew up in a situation that was out of your control, but it shaped you. Did you grow up in a town where the mean girls had even meaner moms who were way too invested in teenage drama? Did you grow up in a family that was divorced or had a lot of trauma? Did that one guy cause you to have trust issues that you're still struggling with years later? Are you working a job to pay your bills, but it's not what you dreamed of when you were young? At some point, life has felt out of control and we've wondered if God can really use us. And, if He can, why would He want to?

But you were there and are here for such a time as this. And we serve a God who can use our past and present to lead us to our blessings. That's the beautiful thing about God: He never fails to use all our twists and turns to lead us to our purpose. Even in those hard seasons and even in our current confusions, God is leading us to where we are meant to be. Your life right now may feel like a lot, and your current environment may seem overwhelming, but God does not waste any season.

Being bold isn't just a characteristic saved for the "girl bosses" of the world. It is meant for you and me. We don't have to be in our dream season or achieve every goal to be bold today. (Keep in mind I'm writing this as I juggle three jobs to pay my bills and feel like I never even have time to brush my hair. But I feel it in my bones that this season is purposeful.) Life may not be going how I want, but I know that, with my God, I am a light. Maybe a busy light, or maybe a small light, but I am a light with the power to shine wherever God places me in this dark world.

Mordecai knew that Esther was not needed to save the Jewish people. In fact, he told Esther, "For if you remain silent at this time, relief and deliverance for the Jews will arise from another place." He knew that no matter what happened, God would figure it out, but he challenged Esther, "And who knows but that you have come to your royal position for such a time as this?" (Est. 4:14).

Esther wasn't the hero; God was. God would deliver the Jewish people no matter what, but He brought Esther to that very place so He could use her to make a difference. Esther was brought to her position to be bold.

So are you, my friend. If God could take Esther and use her position to save the Jewish people, He can also take your job, your annoying early class on Thursdays, your family troubles, your major, or your friendships and bring deliverance to someone there. If Esther could go from being someone without control to using her boldness to stop a genocide, God can use you on your college campus or in your family to point others to Jesus.

Esther risked her life and being liked and ended up being a powerful queen who saved her people. You, too, were created to step into God's best, not to shrivel up to fit (or rather be squeezed) into the world's box for you. Esther had faith, but she did not have control. You may feel like you don't have control over a lot of your circumstances due to a health issue, your family, your past, your looks, or your financial state, but you do have your voice. And your voice gives you the power to be there for "such a time as this." I hope you and I spend more days stepping into God's best and fewer hours stressed about being likeable.

On the days you find yourself overwhelmed and feel like your voice doesn't matter, look up. When you focus on your Creator and Savior, you'll find your voice. Your boldness won't come from your résumé, your self-love, or even your trauma. Your voice comes from the One who breathed life into you and the One who took His final breath for you on the cross. Your voice comes from the One who said, "I love you this much," stretching out His arms to show you, having them nailed to a tree. Your voice comes from the One who rose from the dead and said He would save space for you too. Your voice comes from your Savior.

On the days you feel scared to speak up, scared to apply for that job, and scared of not being liked, look up. Esther didn't care what others thought, because she was following God boldly and faithfully. If she could trust God in a life-or-death situation, then we can surely trust God in our everyday lives.

CHAPTER 2

Five Things Better than Being Too Scared

I DON'T GET HIT ON OFTEN. I'M NOT THE GIRL WHO GETS offered drinks at a bar by handsome guys. That would be my friend Nora. I'm also not the kind of girl who gets chased by a cute and successful twenty-seven-year-old in the middle of downtown Orlando like my friend Ramsey. The guy ran back to compliment Ramsey's dress, then he complimented everything about her. He even said, "I'm flabbergasted by your smile." Some women are just powerful like this.

Though I don't get hit on often, there was one time I remember vividly, when my plane was delayed for four hours. I was stuck waiting for a connecting flight.

After nearly settling for a mediocre meal at the airport Chili's, I walked off, and a man started to chase me. Yes, a guy actually chased me! After an awkward start, he asked for my number. And though I wasn't interested and didn't offer it to him, I was impressed by this guy. I later thought, *Man, that guy wasn't scared of rejection. Go him!*

Then I realized the guy probably *was* scared of rejection, but he chose boldness over being rejected.

I think being scared of rejection is normal. It is scary to be bold. But I believe we should be more scared of missing out on God's best than we are of rejection.

Like many people, I am scared of rejection and scared of being told no. One time, my brother sent me a job opening while I was furloughed, stuck with a mortgage, and struggling for cash. I read the description for the job and laughed. *How sweet my brother thinks I could do this!* There was no way I was even going to get an interview or pass the first round. There was no way they would want me. It was crazy to think my brother had gone from fighting over a remote with me when we were kids to thinking I was qualified for this job.

But when I told him I didn't feel qualified, he laughed. He took my résumé and highlighted parts I could expand on and showed how they met the qualifications. Slowly, I realized that he was right, and I was more qualified than I thought. I applied and made it past the first round. Though I didn't get the job, I was surprised I made it past the first round when I thought I would be completely overlooked.

You're likely scared of something too. A big reason many of us don't step into boldness is because we are scared of rejection, so we choose being fearful over being bold. As simple and silly as some of my previous examples of boldness are, it all starts with a choice. And when I reflect on Esther, a young woman who lived in a society where women, especially of her faith and upbringing, didn't have many choices, I'm thankful and inspired by her choosing boldness.

As we continue to reflect on Esther and how God used her boldness, let's remind ourselves of five things we would rather be than too scared, all based on Esther.

#1 - I would rather be on God's team than too scared.

Just like Mordecai told Esther, deliverance would come for the Jewish people no matter what, but what if God had brought Esther there for such a time as that? I think it's easy to confuse Esther as the hero in this story. I mean, wasn't she the one who boldly told the king she was Jewish and then saved the Jewish people? Yes. But you know who placed her there at that exact time to do this? Our God. God is so good that there are no coincidences.

I wonder what Esther was feeling when she was chosen to be Xerxes' wife and when she moved her whole life into that palace. I wonder how it felt being in that competition where her looks were discussed often. It must have been an odd time, that's for sure, but all of it led her to that moment, to be in the exact place she was meant to be in to live boldly and help God's kingdom.

Maybe you have been through a bad breakup, the loss of your job, family drama, or health issues, or maybe you've also felt like life was out of your control like Esther. It is easy to look back at the hurt, but I want to remind you that in front of you today is your God saying, *I got you this far, for such a time as this.* Instead of being too scared, choose to be on God's team. Choose to walk with the One who turns orphans into queens and you and me into trailblazers for a purpose bigger than ourselves.

In 1 Corinthians 12:12–14, the apostle Paul reminded us that we don't have to do everything ourselves. He wrote, "Just as a body, though one, has many parts, but all its many parts form one body, so it is with Christ. For we were all baptized by one Spirit so as to form one body—whether Jews or Gentiles, slave or free—and we were all given the one Spirit to drink. Even so the body is not made up of one part but of many."

I think we often forget that we don't have to do it all or be it all. In fact, God never asked us to do it all. As believers, we are on God's team, and together we are like a body. Our skills are unique, like an ear is unique and different from an eye, but we work together for God's glory. Mordecai's role was just as important as Esther's. And God was also protecting His people through His role as the Author.

Sometimes boldness comes from realizing you don't have to do all the jobs, just the job the Lord has given you. You can use your position to work together with others for God's glory as you are called to do. We live in a world that tells us to be the hero and to focus on doing it on our own. Jesus never asks you to be bold on your own. Sometimes the boldest thing you can do is look around and ask others to fight with you.

#2 - I would rather be too adventurous than too scared.

What if Esther hadn't been honest about her faith and just let the decree go on? She would've had to watch her cousin, the man who raised her and loved her well, be murdered. She would've had to sit there knowing many of the people she knew growing up were being killed. And she would've had to sit there in the palace knowing she was one of them, but she was denying the God she knew loved her. She would've had to stay married to a king she knew was okay with letting this happen.

That doesn't sound like a great option. However, the option of standing up for her people was probably scarier. Esther risked death, she risked being disliked, and she risked being accused of not knowing her place as a woman in that time. She didn't know how it would end up, but she did know that if she didn't speak up, it would be horrible for the rest of the Jewish people in Persia but safer for her personally. But Esther did speak up.

She chose the option where she didn't know how the king would react or if he would do anything about it. She chose the adventurous route.

I think we have misused the word *adventure*. Adventure doesn't just mean going ziplining in Costa Rica, riding a roller coaster, or taking that crazy road trip with the besties. The definition of *adventurous* according to *Oxford Languages* is "willing to take risks or to try out new methods, ideas, or experiences." Esther is a great example of someone who had to try something new and risky in order to walk in her purpose and to see God's best. She had spent a lot of her life sitting still, being likeable, and being controlled by others. Speaking up wasn't normal for any woman in that time, let alone someone whose people were facing genocide, but she chose the adventure of listening to God's will.

You could try something new and be bold too. Maybe that's something as simple as talking to your neighbor, throwing a dinner party for some peers (even in a season when you feel lonely), leading a Bible study, applying for a certain job, or simply noticing a younger girl and deciding, *I want to be who I needed when I was younger.* Adventure can happen on the Thursday morning you feel overwhelmed and on the Saturday night you stay home. Adventure isn't just trips and flips. It's obediently saying yes to our faithful God and watching Him do something new.

God's best comes to us when we are willing to say yes. You may feel like Esther felt, or maybe you had years of people saying your voice meant nothing. I had a job once where I felt like my voice didn't matter and I wasn't appreciated, and it was hard for me to remember that my voice had power. After a while of feeling like no one would listen, I had to unlearn the fear of my words being rejected. Even if you have felt overlooked or unliked, choose the adventure that comes from speaking up. Be like Esther and realize it is better to be too adventurous than to miss out on God's best because you're too scared.

#3 - I would rather notice my God with me than be too scared.

What makes the book of Esther so interesting is that God's name is never mentioned. I remember someone telling me this once, and I thought, *No way!* But I flipped through the pages and nope, they never name God. However, just because God's name is absent doesn't mean He is. In life we will have seasons where we'll have to be bold in our faith even if we don't feel God. We have to say yes to God's best, even when it feels scary and we can't see God clearly. But we can have faith that He is there even when we don't feel Him.

I think Christians focus on feelings too much. We say, "Bow your heads and feel the Spirit during this worship song." I love worshiping with my hands up if I feel my heart led to reach out in admiration of the Holy Spirit, but when people make their faith to be all about the feelings they received at one camp, one conference, one service, one worship song, or one moment, I believe this is risky. What happens when the chills fade away, and what happens when we face spiritual warfare? I want to notice God, always. You can notice He's there without feeling Him. You can notice He won't abandon you without seeing Him. In Isaiah 43:2 God says, "When you pass through the waters, I will be with you." Feelings are temporary, but our God is eternal.

Noticing God starts with knowing Scripture and knowing God's character. When you know that He's there, you'll see Him in ways you don't expect. You'll notice Him in the kind invitation from a new friend, the confidence and peace you feel at the last minute before a big decision, or, more importantly, in the truth that His Word endures forever (Isa. 40:8). You'll notice that sometimes instead of removing the deep waters, God will allow us to go through them. Then we'll have to choose boldness in them, knowing that our God is with us. The deep waters won't be removed, and we may not feel God, but we'll notice the boldness He gives us to not just go through them but to be led through them by Him.

#4 - I would rather be rejected than too scared.

Sometimes things won't go your way. If you've read my other books, you know I've had my fair share of rejection. Like I said, the man chasing me in the airport was rare. I don't typically get the guy, and I'm not the girl others immediately want to be best friends with. I've tried to be friends with people who didn't care about me, I've shot my shot with men who rejected me, and I've been betrayed by people I thought I could trust. I've applied to jobs I didn't get, and I've taken jobs just to pay my bills. I could write a whole book on all the times I didn't get the job, wasn't liked, was rejected, and felt pushed away. But you know what? I could also write a book on all the times God surprised me and allowed my one little step of boldness to lead me to where I am today. At the age of twelve, I told my parents I was going to write books. At the age of nineteen, I felt led to write books about Jesus because each time I went to Barnes & Noble, it seemed every author was either fifty years older than me and had it all figured out, had literally seen heaven, or was famous for being pretty. I never saw books from young women who were just learning as they went. So I listened to this bold call God gave me to write, and I wrote blogs. After building my website, I reached out to many literary agents (the first step in the publishing process). I was rejected by probably twenty-one agents and ghosted by seventy-five. After each rejection, I learned a little and kept going. All it took was one yes.

I know this sounds like a Christian version of the old quote we've all heard: "You miss 100 percent of the shots you don't take." But let me be honest with you: you'll miss out on 100 percent of God's blessings if you don't listen to His call. You'll miss out on 100 percent of God's good plan for you if you don't lean into being the good. You'll still be rejected. But on the day the job doesn't work out, your boss hates your idea, your social media stats for your business feel small, or you get rejected by the guy, I pray you look up. Your God is working all things for your good, including the rejection (Rom. 8:28).

Like Elle's professor in the movie *Legally Blonde* says, "If you're going to let one stupid [person] ruin your life, then you're not the girl I thought you were," I feel like maybe God looks at us and says, *If you're going to let the fear of rejection stop you from being bold, then you're not the daughter I know you can be.*

Be more scared of missing out on God's best than you are of being rejected.

#5 - I would rather be a good listener to God than be too scared.

Want to know why we so often aren't bold? We start listening to the "what-ifs" instead of the "what could God allow this to be?" The "what-ifs" are dangerous because they often distract us from remembering who God is. God is our leader, shepherd, and faithful lifeline who cares for us, saves us, and walks with us. It is easy to forget those things when we start listening to our fears. It is easier to talk ourselves out of being bold when we're drowning out God's voice that is saying, *Trust Me.*

I want to be a good listener to God. There's a spiritual gift called *discernment* that I've started to pray for more of this past year. I want to discern God's best and have the wisdom to walk away from anything that is causing me to miss out on Him. I want to discern God's voice and hear Him more than I hear my fears. I want to discern God's will so I can walk boldly in it instead of fearing it. I want to discern His Word so well that I praise Him when I am rejected and not liked, instead of overthinking and playing the "what-if" game. May you and I be better at listening to God and stop giving fear and the world a place in our minds. Colossians 3:1–2 says, "Since, then, you have been raised with Christ, set your hearts on things above, where Christ is, seated at the right hand of God. Set your minds on things above, not on earthly things." May we set our minds on things above so we can't help but listen to His will.

Sometimes, I think we are bad at listening to God in the mundane—on the Thursdays before that meeting with that boss or on the Mondays when we're overwhelmed with school. It is easy to set our hearts on that degree, that grade, that promotion, that relationship, or even that acceptance from a certain person. But those things will fail us. When we set our hearts on things above and align our thoughts and minds with God, we not only hear Him more clearly but we aren't afraid to step into God's goodness.

Here's what I wish so badly for you and me: I wish we would be like Esther and see the risk but also see our God. I pray we see the risk of being unliked, rejected, or unsuccesful, but instead of fearing that rejection we fear missing out on God's will more. I hope when I am old and gray, I'll be able to share about all the adventurous moments I had with my God that started with a simple yes. I hope I can share how I was bold and how my God was always faithful. I hope I can also share the times it didn't go my way but how I didn't care. I may have been hurt a little, but I saw how God used every twist and turn to help lead me to my good.

So, on the days you're scared, I pray you remember our God is good. There will be rejection and fear, but there will also always be miracles and glory. I hope we both know that the risk is worth the reward when it comes to being bold.

PART 2

What Will They Think If I'm a Leader?

She held court under the Palm of Deborah between Ramah and Bethel in the hill country of Ephraim, and the Israelites went up to her to have their disputes decided.

JUDGES 4:5

CHAPTER 3

Learn from Deborah

ONE TIME, I WENT ON A BLIND DATE WITH A GUY BECAUSE a new friend encouraged me to. She meant well, and the guy wasn't awful, but he repeatedly said something along the lines of, "I can't believe you're not fat, like I was so sure you would be."

I finally responded out of frustration, "Yes, I don't look the way you expected. Can we move on?"

If you know anything about my past, you know body image is something I've struggled with. I've skipped meals, made myself throw up, and done a lot of unhealthy things to gain control and to please others with my looks. Maybe he thought talking about my body was a compliment, but I think most women would agree it made him sound like a jerk. He obsessed over how I looked without knowing I've overthought how others view my body my entire life. His comments about what he had thought of me beforehand only made me stress the next day about what I ate.

But the truth is, I didn't stand up for myself or other women any more than a single comment. Although I didn't need to chew him out, I could've stood up for myself.

When someone annoys me, hurts me, or hurts someone else, I have a tendency to handle conflict in one of three ways:

- I ignore it and smile. I try to move past it without saying any truth. I sit pretty, move along, and try not to discomfort anyone.
- I make a snappy comment. I handle rude with rude. I don't use self-control, and chances are, my response is from an

unhealthy place of built-up frustration and is not meant for just one person.

- I cry. Ugly cry. Conflict is not my specialty. Some people who know me think I'm a tough cookie, but the truth is that those who know me best know my tears are mixed with snot and loud breathing when I'm really upset.

I think we, as women, are scared to be the leader or stand up confidently in a conversation, at a job, in our families, and in the kingdom of God. We think that being bold means we have to assume the role of men. We think we aren't qualified or given authority to step up and say the truth. And this doesn't just apply to a date when an offensive comment is being shared; it could also relate to your job.

I remember when I was regularly shot down for five months at my job for any idea I presented. It took a while for them to simply listen to me, and I wanted to quit by that point. But I kept going. Perhaps you think that you're unqualified to step up in your sorority when you notice rush isn't truly looking out for girls but is just an atmosphere of gossip and judgment, or in church when you hear people talking down to others and not calling them up and inviting them in.

It is easy for us to believe the lies: I'm not capable of handling this right. I don't have the perfect words, so maybe I shouldn't say anything or I should wait until it bothers me more. It is better for me to be quiet and stay liked. Or perhaps one of the biggest lies: That's a man's job.

When I was in fourth grade, I wanted to be the president. Not the president of a club or Girl Scouts—I wanted to be the president of the United States. I was also going through a suit phase at this point. I loved suits with skirts and wore them to church like I was Hillary Clinton or Nikki Haley. I looked like I was ready for the White House, not recess. The best part of my wanting to be the president was that whenever I told my teachers at my public school in Louisiana, they always believed in me. I knew there were no women presidents, but I never doubted myself. The people around me didn't doubt me either.

I never became president of the United States (at least not yet), and I traded my two-piece suits for funky pants and felt called to speak and write about Jesus. But even then I stopped for a while because, well, I didn't see any women doing this. I didn't see any normal women even writing books, only famous ones or Miss America–types. I thought I was too ordinary, and it wasn't my place as a woman to share my thoughts on Scripture. Suddenly, the ten-year-old who believed her teachers when they told her she could be anything was gone. She had traded in her crazy faith for realistic beliefs.

Then I met Deborah.

Deborah is a woman in the Old Testament who continually surprises me. She was the only female judge of Israel in the Bible, which means she was high up politically even as a woman. I think so often we tell women they can speak truth only to other women, while men can speak to women and men, which doesn't make sense. But Deborah was a prophet and a judge in Israel, and everyone listened to her.

Deborah's name in Hebrew meant "bee," as in an insect bee. This stood by her character because prophets and judges were followed and swarmed like queen bees with their colonies. A bee can have a strong sting but sweet honey, and this was a character-istic of Deborah's leadership. Even though Deborah was faithful and kind, she was also fierce and not afraid to stand up for others, her colony, or herself. Bees work together for the common good of their colony, and what does a faithful leader hope to establish in their community? A group that works together for God's glory. And let's be honest: bees are insects. They aren't the main characters. They focus on their community. But Deborah was humble even though she was a leader, so her name fit her well.

Her job was also a doozy. I have a difficult time confronting a date who's making rude comments, yet Deborah helped resolve many people's problems. She spoke into the lives of many in her area. As a judge, she would sit under a tree, and the Israelites (citizens she ruled over) would line up to hear her ruling. They came to her for guidance. They knew that she would pray and that her decisions would honor God's Word. But what is also cool is that Deborah was a military leader. Back in her day, and even still today, a military leader is in charge of the safety of the residents. If a military leader isn't strong, then the country as a whole suffers.

One day, Deborah summoned a man named Barak to lead ten thousand men to Mount Tabor and begin battle (Judg. 4:6). God commanded her to do this to protect her people. Barak, in verse 8, said he would go only if she would go. It is hard to know if this was because he didn't trust that this was a good idea or if he was scared and wanted her to help. Many believe Barak was being a coward and not stepping up fully to the role he was given, so Deborah had to step up more. But Deborah's response to him was interesting and prophetic to how the story would end. Deborah agreed to lead with Barak but said, "But because of the course you are taking, the honor will not be yours, for the LORD will deliver Sisera into the hands of a woman" (v. 9).

Sisera was the commander of the Canaanite army, the army the Israelites would be battling. During that time, killing the commander of the enemy's army was a glorious event that was widely celebrated by the victors. Naturally, we as readers assume Deborah would be the woman who ended up killing Sisera, but when the Israelites (led by Deborah and Barak) won the battle, Sisera fled and went to hide in the tent of a woman named Jael, and she killed him. This fulfilled Deborah's prophecy of a woman killing the commander.

You're probably like, *Wow. Deborah was a rock star, but how does that relate to me?* Here's the truth: there's a Deborah in all of us waiting to come out. We may not have the gift of prophecy or politics, and most of us won't be military leaders, but we can all learn three things from Deborah's story.

Deborah wasn't afraid to step up and go where God called her.

Sometimes as women, we might be called by God to do something out of the ordinary. Whether God is calling you to talk about Jesus with a friend, start a website, open a business, or be honest with your boss about the company's culture, it is important to listen for God's call. Deborah didn't wonder, *Is it my place as a woman to be doing this?* And let's be clear, times were a lot harder for women then than they are now.

First John 2:17 says, "And the world is passing away along with its desires, but whoever does the will of God abides forever" (esv). Deborah was not fearful of others not listening to her as a woman or not liking her. She wasn't concerned about someone thinking she was bossy. She wasn't worried about outshining her husband (yes, she was married). She wasn't scared about being different. She was focused on doing the will of God.

It is hard in college, on a date, in your job, and even while raising a family to step up in times of stress, trial, and burdens to choose obedience in God's will. It is often easier to point to someone else and say, "You got this one." But that is the beautiful part about God's story. He wants women to rise up like Deborah and be a part of His plan. He wants us to be on His team. We may not be liked, others may not trust us, but when we are obedient and following God's will, we are purposeful and bold.

Barak put his faith in Deborah.
Deborah put her faith in God.

Barak is believed by many to have doubted God and trusted in Deborah instead. That is why he said he would go only if Deborah went with him, because in this moment of battle, he didn't fully trust God. He didn't see God before him like Deborah did. Maybe he was just scared of the battle.

I don't think Barak was the only one to have doubted God in this time, but how Deborah handled him is inspiring. She didn't say a sassy comment or kick him out for not trusting fully in God. She knew God had chosen Barak to be there, even if he didn't see God, and he was chosen just as much as she was. But she basically told him, "Hey, you're going to miss out on something cool like being the one to receive the honor for killing the Canaanite commander, and because you're a coward, a woman will rise up."

Deborah didn't allow Barak's doubt to be contagious like we

all know it can be. I remember in fifth grade someone told our class Santa wasn't real. Those of us who still believed in Santa went home and asked our parents if this was true, and each day someone else came back and added more doubt. I've also seen this happen on a bigger, adult-sized scale. All it takes is one person to say they doubt God for you to start doubting God too. All it takes is one person in college to say you're missing out on the college experience if you don't go to this party, participate in this lifestyle, or try these things. All it takes is one boyfriend to say if you don't do this, you don't love me. All it takes is one boss or coworker to make you feel like your contributions in the meeting aren't important. Unfortunately, if I had been in Deborah's place and Barak had come to me a little scared and said, "I'll go only if you'll go because this is an insane idea," I would've possibly backed out and changed my mind. I would've wanted Barak to think I was capable and thought all the realistic thoughts through. But Deborah responded that God would do it, and now He'd use a woman.

You're going to have doubters, haters, people who don't think you're capable, and people who don't think your God is capable. They'll call you crazy, and they'll try to convince you to doubt yourself. I mean, Elle Woods had Warner, Taylor Swift was still cheated on, and you have that one girl from high school who still talks bad about you or that guy at work who gives you the stink eye in your meeting. You will have doubters and haters. But what will your response be? Let it be one that reflects obedience to God and not one that's about having a good clapback or giving in to the doubt. Friend, I hope you can look at the naysayers, haters, or people who just don't like you and say confidently that your battle isn't about convincing them it's going to work. Don't waste time fighting the distraction beside you. Instead, suit up and walk boldly into your purpose.

> **When people make you, as a woman, feel**
> **like an object meant to please others,**
> **remind them you're a warrior.**

Deborah isn't the only woman in this story who did something remarkable. In Judges 4, Jael got the glory of killing the Canaanite commander. I know you may be thinking, *Yikes . . . murder is a little hard.* This war was for the protection of Israel and to keep Deborah in power. There are also many questions as to why Jael felt compelled to kill the Canaanite commander, when the commander believed she was on his side and even escaped there for his protection. We don't know why she killed the commander, but we do know the Israelites were protected and Deborah's prophecy was fulfilled. We know God was on their side. We know Jael was a warrior for fulfilling God's plan and Deborah was a warrior for listening to God Himself, even in the midst of a crazy season. I believe God purposefully used two women who were doubted and gave them the jobs of leading, prophesying, and defeating the enemy in this battle for a reason. The Bible was written during a time when the culture didn't respect women, but God used the events in Judges 4 to remind us that women are capable and fierce. We are called to be leaders, and God's glory can shine through us.

I can now think back to that date's remarks about my body and laugh. What did he think I was? A jacket he ordered online? We as women are not objects to be enjoyed or products to be reviewed by men. We are warriors, capable of being obedient to God, leading others, and defeating the lies and battles we face. Our purpose is to fight the fight and lead others to God's obedience, not to sit and smile as others overlook us.

I know you have your own battle right now. I also know you have something God is calling you to. It is easy to listen to the lies from the doubters and those who don't trust a woman's ability, but you must focus on listening to your God. May we be like Deborah, the right kind of queen bee, not the queen bee we see in an old 2000s movie. May we be strong in our fight but sweet like honey.

CHAPTER 4

Five Things Deborah Sang About

I FINALLY THREW AWAY MY JEANS THIS WEEK. YOU MAY be thinking, *Why would you throw away your jeans?* So let me tell you.

These jeans were my jeggings from American Eagle in 2013. They were stretchy enough to last longer than other jeans and even fit for a while post–high school. I truly believe if the world ended, our American Eagle jeans, Crocs, and fire ants would all survive. These jeans had been sitting in my closet for some time. But the real reason I kept these jeans was not their durability. It was because I always hoped to fit into them again one day.

The truth is, these size 2 jeans fit when I had an eating disorder. I shouldn't be longing to fit in them again. I shouldn't waste precious closet space with these jeans from an unhealthy era. But I kept them longer than I should have. Why? Because they were my priority. I hoped for a few things:

- Being as skinny as my seventeen-year-old self. (I cried trying on homecoming dresses at seventeen because I felt fat, but I hold up these jeans now and wish I could fit in them.)
- Being what I thought others would think was more attractive.
- Being someone I could never again be.

Many of us gain weight after high school because our hips are literally different. We are now more capable of giving birth to a child than we were at age fifteen. I work out four times a week, eat my greens, and do my squats, but my body will never be able to fit in those size 2 jeans again. And that's not a bad thing. I could bear children now with these hips if it is God's will. The same legs I complain about have carried me through many college campuses where I got to share the gospel. So what kind of torture was it to keep those jeans around?

And it's not just these crusty, out-of-style but tiny jeans I've kept around too long. I've kept some guys around too long because, well, it was comforting and they liked me. They were not good for my growth, but I was bored and insecure and kept them around. This only stopped me from moving on and growing in my purpose. I've kept toxic friendships without good boundaries, and a job that made me overwhelmed. I didn't want to disappoint anyone, so instead I disappointed my mental health.

I didn't even get counseling for my eating disorder until I relapsed. Keep in mind this was after I had written a whole book on insecurity. I wanted to think I had found the cure, but I didn't want to go through the true battle. I wanted to think the battle was over, but really I was in denial that God was calling me to work through my issues.

I think we all have many battles we have to work through. Whether that's our addiction to pleasing people, our family trauma, our relationship abuse, the relationship we need to walk away from, our job stress, our doubts in our faith, insecurities from comments made years ago, or anything else, we have to show up to the fight.

In Judges 5, we see the story of Deborah again, but something is different: it is in the form of a song. This song is about how she showed up for the literal fight, and I believe it can be a battle plan for each of us. Let's dig into this song.

1. Deborah and Barak praised God for the leaders and people who were willing to offer themselves.

To start off Judges 5, we see an appreciation for anyone willing to be used by God. Judges 5:1–2 says, "On that day Deborah and Barak son of Abinoam sang this song: 'When the princes in Israel take the lead, when the people willingly offer themselves—praise the LORD!'" Notice that Deborah and Barak didn't praise the leaders or the commanders; they praised the Lord. They celebrated themselves and the ten thousand men who went into battle but gave the glory to God. They appreciated the willingness of others to do God's will. There are plenty of leaders in our world who aren't even willing to hear God out, so praise God for those who are even stepping their toes into obedience.

For your battle plan to work through any of your past trauma or trials, first praise God for all those alongside you willing to show up to the fight. Praise God for the leaders in your life and the leader you will grow to become.

2. They remembered all that God had done for them in the past.

Judges 5:3–5 continues, "Hear this, you kings! Listen, you rulers! I, even I, will sing to the LORD; I will praise the LORD, the God of Israel, in song. When you, LORD, went out from Seir, when you marched from the land of Edom, the earth shook, the heavens poured, the clouds poured down water. The mountains quaked before the LORD, the One of Sinai, before the LORD, the God of Israel."

Something we notice here is that Deborah and Barak reflected on all God had done to protect Israel. Before the battle, they remembered that God had saved them before and He would do it again. When Deborah sang, "the mountains quaked before the LORD," she acknowledged that God was more powerful than anything and would be powerful again. Deborah displayed her discernment in recognizing what God had done in the past for Israel, and she sang praises to Him when she reflected on it. Notice that she didn't sing about the hardships and give glory to the trauma; she sang about their victories and gave glory to her God.

After this, in verses 6–8, we see that Deborah remembered the painful Canaanite oppression. Before she fought the Canaanites, she remembered they were not good for her. When you're battling your trials, addiction, pain, or obsessive need to please, you may also have to remind yourself not just that your God is powerful but that the worldly thing you're obsessing over isn't good for you.

For your battle plan to work through any of your past trauma or trials, you need to remember all God has done for you. I get it—maybe you look back and see only tears in your past. But look at where your feet are planted. Praise God for bringing you this far. There were days you thought the breakup would break you, the lies would destroy you, the gossip would tear you down, and the abandonment would make you forever lonely. But see where your feet are? God carried you this far, and He will do it again.

3. They recounted the victory, then recounted who helped them and who did not.

In Judges 5:10–18, we see two things happen: Deborah

began to sing and celebrate the victory, then she remembered who helped and who didn't.

For your battle plan to work through any of your past trauma or trials, you need to recount the small victories. Recount the moment you finally walked away from the party, the bad relationship, the addiction, or the insecurity—and praise God. Then reflect on what helped you get there, who helped you grow, and who wasn't on your team. It is important to create an environment that helps you grow instead of one that causes you to miss out on God's best.

4. They praised those who were faithful to God.

In Judges 5:24–27, we read of how Jael killed Sisera, who came as a guest in her tent. It is important to note how she was praised by Deborah. Jael went against the standards and customs on how to treat guests normally. But as judge of Israel Deborah praised Jael for killing Sisera, because Jael knew her faith in God's plan was more important than any tradition.

For your battle plan to work through any of your past trauma or trials, sometimes you may have to fight head-first against your trial or pain. I am not saying you should kill anyone, and I'm also not giving you permission or praise for vandalizing your ex-boyfriend's property, but I am showing you that sometimes you'll have to walk away. Is walking away normally the kind thing to do? No. But we can often recognize when God's will is for us to walk away. Maybe you need to stand up to a boss or a coworker, or maybe you need to leave a toxic job that causes you doubt. If so, do it with grace, but trust in the God who calls you. Work hard, love big, but listen to God's voice more than you listen to what others want you to do or what has normally been expected of you.

5. They remembered who the true Enemy was.

Deborah's song in Judges 5 ends with a beautiful verse: "So may all your enemies perish, LORD! But may all who love you be like the sun when it rises in its strength" (v. 31).

Notice that this lyric in her song says, "may all *your* enemies perish," not "my" enemies. My enemies include a boy who rejected me, another boy who cheated on me, a mean lady I once worked with, and the girl who always talks bad about me. God's enemies are Satan and any of the lies he tells us. Deborah's song ends with a beautiful call for all who love God to be like the sun when it rises. The sun rises each morning, gracefully and on schedule. The sun has moments when clouds block it and rain distracts others from feeling it, but it is always there, shining and fulfilling its purpose.

For your battle plan to work through any of your past trauma or trials, remember who the true Enemy is. Don't cheer for your name to be known but for God's will to be done. Don't cheer for your boldness to help *you*; cheer for your boldness to result in God's glory. And on the hard days, ask God to help you shine like the sun and rise each morning ready to be bright and help others see the glory of God around them. The sun's purpose isn't to please, and on some days, others may think it is too bright. The sun's purpose is to shine continually. It doesn't stop shining to please others. Keep faithfully shining the glory of your God.

Whether you're fighting the world's expectations for you or something else, it is my prayer that you learn to be bold and sing your song. Like Deborah, we each have a song that tells a story of the hardships we face, what God has done, and what God will do. There's victory to be won, and your story isn't over yet. Keep fighting, keep singing, and shine bright.

PART 3

What Will They Think If I've Made Mistakes?

Sarah said, "God has brought me laughter, and everyone who hears about this will laugh with me."

GENESIS 21:6

She gave this name to the LORD who spoke to her: "You are the God who sees me," for she said, "I have now seen the One who sees me."

GENESIS 16:13

CHAPTER 5

*Learn from Sarah
and Hagar*

THE NIGHT AFTER GRADUATION, I DID WHAT MANY people do after they graduate from college: I went to the same bar I'd gone to all four years with the same people I'd always gone with. It was the place for me that brought up flashbacks to funny memories, awful memories (I'm not a cute crier, so "awful" means a lot of tears and snot), and memories that made me who I am today.

I remember one particular conversation I had with my best guy friend that night. We had shared so many memories in college, but our relationship was strictly platonic, and he had a girlfriend who was one of the kindest people I knew. They were cute, and I had heard a rumor they were getting engaged soon. I remember looking him in the eye and saying, "If I'm not invited to your wedding, I will be mad."

Though he beat around the bush when I brought up the rumor, he confirmed that when he gets married, I would most definitely be invited. And I'd be seated at a higher-ranked table. I was a table three kind of friend for him, not table sixteen in the back corner.

But during my seventeen-hour drive home, I heard from people that they had broken up. I remember laughing. I cared for him, and though I never pictured us as anything more than friends, I would be lying if I said I had never thought about what we would have been if he were single. But that wasn't the case and I had simply embraced how lucky I was to have a friend like him. The fact that I heard the news of their breakup on the day I was driving home from Texas to Florida did make me laugh. I called my best friend and said, "Well, we know we were not meant to be. We didn't even have one day together being single."

We stayed close and talked often. And then one day after years of friendship he told me he thought he was in love with me. Although we kind of tried a dating relationship, things ultimately didn't work out, and that's okay. He's a great guy, and I'm thankful for his friendship. We just weren't meant to be.

I used to think, *Maybe there is such a thing as being with the right person at the wrong time.* But the truth is, there's only God's time. We can try to make things work all we want, but the reason things don't work is because they aren't God's will.

There is a well-known woman in the Bible named Sarah, whom we can all learn from. She was married to Abraham, who was part of the family line that led to Jesus. In Genesis 17, God told Abraham that he would be the father of many nations, even though he and Sarah were of old age and had no children. God said Sarah would give birth to a son and that she would be "the mother of nations; kings of peoples will come from her" (v. 16).

How did Abraham react to this news, across many chapters of God telling him that he and his wife, both in their nineties, would bear a son? He fell face-forward and laughed. Keep in mind, this was a covenant that God was telling Abraham about in these chapters.

In that culture it was an honor for one's name to continue on through a son. Although Abraham and Sarah knew God had promised them that they would have heirs, they tried to create their own plan in their own timing. Sarah thought there was no way she would be able to be a part of this promise because of her age, so she arranged for her slave to sleep with Abraham in order to give him a son and therefore a legacy. Although it may seem odd to us for Abraham to use a slave to bear the child that would be his heir, it was a common tradition back then.

Although this didn't make it right, it is important to see how the culture affected Sarah's decision. After her slave, Hagar, got pregnant from Abraham, Sarah became jealous and began mistreating her. Again, in Genesis 17, God came to Abraham. He plainly assured him that Sarah was a part of the plan and the impossible would happen, yet Abraham laughed.

In Genesis 18, Sarah also heard from the Lord that she would bear Abraham's child. Although she didn't fall facedown like Abraham, she laughed in her thoughts and doubts. She thought, "After I am worn out and my lord is old, will I now have this pleasure?" (v. 12). The Lord replied to her laughter, "Why did Sarah laugh and say, 'Will I really have a child, now that I am old?' Is anything too hard for the LORD? I will return to you at the appointed time next year, and Sarah will have a son" (vv. 13–14). God called Sarah out for her laughter, and she lied to God. But God told her she would give birth to a son in a year.

Finally, the impossible happened, and Sarah became pregnant and gave birth to her son, Isaac, even in her old age. She said, "God has brought me laughter, and everyone who hears about this will laugh with me." Then she added, "Who would have said to Abraham that Sarah would nurse children? Yet I have borne him a son in his old age" (Gen. 21:6–7).

Abraham and Sarah first laughed at God in doubt, then they laughed in joy. There are three things I think we can learn from Sarah in this passage:

Sarah learned God's plans don't always make sense.

Even though she first doubted, God never gave up on her seeing that He was in control.

When we doubt that God can do something, we unsuccessfully try to make it happen on our own accord instead of God's. Sarah wasn't bold at first. When Sarah longed to provide Abraham with a son, she was human, jealous, and doubtful, but she became bold.

You may not feel bold today, and you may struggle to trust that God can do it, but allow your laughter to become laughter of joy instead of laughter of doubt. There is beauty found in admiring Sarah's story, because she learned. She wasn't trusting at first, but God was persistent and patient. She tried to make it happen in a way that made sense, but God showed her and told her that trusting in God leads to blessings. Being bold isn't always being the hero and breaking glass ceilings. Sometimes the boldest thing you can do is let God be God and trust that He will make a way. I want you to know God is pursuing you. God is persistent at reminding you that you belong in this story.

God promised Abraham and Sarah that Abraham would be the father of many nations, establishing a covenant that many generations would come from him and that his family name would be passed down. This was the ultimate honor and blessing. Sarah wanted this blessing to happen but didn't think it could involve her. Scripture tells us she was well past the years of childbearing. She was sure there was no way this covenant could involve her. But it did. God was persistent in showing her. Finally, Sarah was bold enough to let God be God.

As much as I want to focus on all the times women in the

Bible were bold, we have to remember they were still sinful people whose lives were messy. The women in the Bible were human. They got jealous, doubted, and sometimes they even lied to God like Sarah did when asked if she was laughing. Sarah wasn't bold at first but became bold. You and I aren't perfect, and in the past, we've tried to put a comma in the chapters where God wanted a period. We've tried to put a period when God wanted the sentence to go on. We are not the authors of our stories, but so often we try to steal the pen from God and write it anyway. We think we are helping, but God is good at being God. He doesn't need our help; He wants our trust and obedience. He wants to bless us and show us miracles, but we have to trust Him to be God.

If you're not bold right now and have tried to control your situations one too many times, Sarah gets it. But when she finally trusted God and watched Him do the impossible, she laughed with joy. Laughing with joy is way more fun than laughing with doubt. If God can help Sarah go from being someone who tried to control her life by manipulating things to bearing a child when she was ninety, then surely He can help you be bold at your job, in your friendships, in your classes, in your service, and even in your dating life as well.

Sarah wasn't an afterthought for God.

Sarah doubted whether the covenant of Abraham being the father of many nations would include her—to the point where she made her own plans. We, too, often doubt whether God's promise involves us, but there will be miracles that involve us, not just shown to us.

I often doubt God wants to use me. I often think God orchestrates big things for His big kingdom, but I'm just a sidekick or an afterthought in His story. Sarah felt this way, too, but she was actually the one who would bear Isaac. She was the one who would experience this unexpected miracle. She was included. God wanted Sarah, despite her imperfections and sins. He wanted to use her. And God wants to use you. Be bold and walk in this truth so you can trust you won't just be on the sidelines watching miracles happen. God wants your life to be a walking miracle that inspires others if you're bold enough to trust Him.

God is always at work.

There's no such thing as too late, too young, or the right person at the wrong time. If it's God's will, you won't miss it. Even if you've doubted before, it doesn't mean you've forever missed out on God's best.

I wonder how Sarah felt when she saw other women her age who already had kids and many generations in their families. She probably felt like she'd missed out. People probably talked negatively about her and made up rumors that she was "cursed." She had many years of waiting. She surely felt worse than silly me driving to Florida thinking I might have missed out on "the one." Maybe Sarah thought that chapter in her life had closed. Maybe you are sitting here thinking it is too late for you to find true friends, have a job you feel purposeful at, start that dream business, pour into others, or even fall in love. I want to be married one day, and on the days that I get sad, I act like Sarah and try to force things that aren't God's best, or

I look back and think, *Well, I missed out.* But that's not true. It is not too late for you and me to live out God's will. God's will always leads us to where we are meant to be. We are not powerful enough to rewrite His will. Don't get me wrong: we can disobey and avoid seeing His will, but when we are walking in boldness in the present, there will be peace. There will be trust. There will sometimes be doubt, but there will always be a God who works all things together for our good (Rom. 8:28). No, you're not promised your dream job or even a husband, but you serve a God who hears your desires, listens to them, and wants to lead you to His best.

When I first read about Sarah, I thought, *Wow, cool. God used her.*

Then I read it again and thought about Hagar, the poor slave Sarah offered up to her husband. The poor young woman Sarah eventually had her husband banish. The poor girl who had to run away from Sarah's jealousy. Then I got mad. Why would God choose to use Sarah for something so cool when she wasn't the nicest girl in the world?

I mean, it felt like I was watching the mean girl in high school end up on homecoming court. Or watching a jerk ex-boyfriend find a great girl after you. It doesn't seem fair.

But the truth is, we are all messy like Sarah. She lied and was jealous. She doubted God. Sarah wasn't a perfect girl who always did as she should; she was disobedient. Honestly, that is me. Maybe as you read this you think, *Well, I've made a lot of bad choices so there's no way God would want to use someone like me.* Or maybe you know you've been the one who has hurt others, been jealous, and doubted God. But God can use anyone for His purpose. God doesn't care about your past; He cares that you repent and follow Him. God doesn't just want to love you; He wants to give you miracles and blessings.

Be bold enough to wait for God's will. Don't settle along the way for a mediocre story written by a doubtful you. It is okay if something you were excited about didn't work out as soon as you wished. It is okay if you didn't graduate on time, move out by twenty-five, pay off your debt by thirty, or have kids before thirty-five. Work hard, wait on the Lord, and live in your present, expectant of miracles to come from your faithful God. I like to think one day I'll be older and hopefully wiser, watching TV, probably laughing and remembering all the days I thought I was missing out, when in reality God was leading me to His best. And until that day, I'll choose trust and boldness over trying to write the story God has already written.

And when you see miracles, when you get the job, when you meet someone who loves you like Jesus, and when people ask how it happened, I hope you laugh. I hope you laugh because you know God did. I hope you see that your boldness led you to the unexpected. I hope you laugh at how faithful your God is and how you were silly to ever doubt Him.

CHAPTER 6

Five Things God Sees in Me

THE COVID-19 PANDEMIC WAS TOUGH FOR A LOT OF US.
I went from being constantly around people to feeling lonely. I
went from thinking I could plan my life and be on top of it all to
realizing how quickly everything could change.

If you read my second book, *Is It Just Me?*, you may remember
that the second week into the COVID-19 lockdown I was furloughed for a while right after buying a house. I was so proud of
having my own house, but owning a home definitely required me
to have a job. And let's be real: no one saw a pandemic coming.

After I was furloughed, I cried. I was sitting in my small but
expensive (for me) house, crying about the job that just broke
up with me, overwhelmed about the pandemic and my bills,
wondering if anyone could see me. I felt alone, but I also felt
like people were seeing only my failures. I was embarrassed and
felt like people saw me as a sad, injured puppy, not the real me.
And I felt like I didn't have time to really process my emotions.
I had bills to pay. I texted every mother in the Orlando area and
offered to babysit. Did I necessarily feel comfortable babysitting
in a pandemic, when at that point we knew nothing about it? No.
But I, like many other Americans, had no choice but to find any
way possible to pay my bills.

Throughout the pandemic, I was also worried about my
grandmother. I was the relative who lived closest to her, so I
wanted to check in to be sure she was okay. She was losing her
eyesight at the time, so she occasionally needed someone to check
on her television, help with little things, and make sure she had
groceries.

During one visit, I didn't hug her but still hung out with her. She knows how to make me feel seen even in the midst of pain. However, when I returned home, I discovered that one of my roommates who had just moved in tested positive for COVID. I realized that before I left for my grandmother's, I'd made the silly mistake of thinking the antibody test was a COVID test, so I'd taken the wrong one before I drove to see her. I'd lost my job, and then when I had tried to help my grandmother, I might have risked her life. Praise Jesus that I didn't give it to her, but I still sat on my bed that day feeling worse than before. My roommate's positive test meant I couldn't babysit, and money would be even tighter than it already was.

My mom talked to me on the phone about it all. She said, "Well, we all know you're not a hugger, Grace, so that made me feel better." I laughed, but she was right. I'm the one at holidays who has to mentally prepare for hugs. Don't get me wrong; I'm bubbly, decently kind, and spunky, but I am not into physical touch.

After my mom said this, I remember thinking, *I may hate hugs, but I have never in my life needed a hug as much as I do right now.* After I was done quarantining for COVID and was positive for antibodies, I visited my parents since I knew at that point it was unlikely I could give them COVID. And I did something out of character—I hugged them. My dad is like me and a little awkward when it comes to emotion, but after months of crying to him on the phone about being furloughed, feeling so hurt, alone, and broken during this season, we hugged. After months of feeling alone, living alone, and struggling to find peace, I felt seen and loved.

You may have felt broken before, or maybe you feel broken

right now. Maybe you hide your emotions and struggle because you don't want to feel needy. Maybe you feel like you have to be the strong one. Maybe you're scared others will judge you if they know that even you, the strong one, sometimes need to feel seen, known, and loved.

Here's the truth: bold women still have hard days; bold women struggle with feeling lonely; bold women can feel hurt; bold women still need to feel seen.

I think we all want to be seen and loved, especially in our hardest seasons. Maybe for you that is because the job you have overlooks you. Maybe you feel overlooked by your peers or you are struggling to make genuine friendships in your current season. Maybe your family has made it hard for you to think anyone could know you and want you. Maybe the breakup still makes you question your worth. Maybe your singleness makes you question whether anyone sees you.

We talked about Sarah in the last chapter, but now I want to talk about her slave, Hagar. Hagar was the woman Sarah instructed to sleep with her husband in order to get pregnant so her husband could have a son. Remember, this was normal back then, but that doesn't make it right. Sarah planned this when she didn't trust that God's promise involved her. After Hagar got pregnant, even though that's exactly what Sarah's plan had been, Sarah became jealous of her. She treated Hagar so awfully she ran away. However, an angel called to Hagar and told her, "Go back to your mistress and submit to her" (Gen. 16:9). The angel then instructed Hagar to name her child Ishmael, which means "God hears," and the angel promised that her child would be a "wild donkey of a man" (v. 12).

That might sound silly to you and me, but to Hagar, being

a "wild donkey of a man" meant her son would be free and untamed. He would have freedom and would not be a slave like she was. However, God did say he would "be against everyone and everyone's hand against him" (v. 12). His life wouldn't be easy, but he would have freedom. Freedom was precious to Hagar, something she didn't fully understand. She was a slave, and now she was in the desert feeling hopeless and bound to loneliness. God met her in the middle of her hopelessness and despair and offered her this promise. She went from being stranded alone in the desert to being assured that God was there for her.

Hagar responded by saying, "You are the God who sees me . . . I have now seen the One who sees me" (Gen. 16:13). How beautiful is that—that in despair, through late nights as a runaway slave in the desert, and after years of being overlooked, used, and hurt, she realized that she had a God who saw her? She realized that even in her despair and on her darkest day, God was there. He wasn't far away in the clouds or just chilling on the streets of gold; He was sitting with her. He saw her, He knew her, and He was with her. So she listened. She obeyed even when it meant she had to go back to a place of hurt.

Boldness isn't comfortable.

Boldness isn't always without tears.

Boldness doesn't always take place in a joyful moment. Boldness isn't exclusive to the celebrities who talk about Jesus while accepting their Grammy. Boldness sometimes takes place in your low, in the hurt, and in the icky. Boldness is walking away from what's comfortable and choosing to be closer to God rather than safe.

Boldness can look different for each of us, but you can't be bold unless you realize that your God sees you. And when you realize God sees you, it feels like a hug from someone who cares. I'm lucky to have an earthly father who loves me well and gave me that hug after that hard season, but I know many of you may not have that. I want you, wherever you are right now, to look up. Your God sees you. Look around you; you're not alone, and your God stands with you. Feel your heartbeat. Your God isn't finished with you yet. Your despair may be real. You may hate hugs. Your pain may feel never-ending, but maybe, like Hagar, God is calling you to be bold and continue walking in this season. And you aren't walking alone.

What's interesting is that Hagar went back to Sarah and Abraham, and later she got kicked out with Ishmael. Sarah did that in Genesis 21 because Ishmael was mocking Isaac, and she demanded that Abraham not allow Ishmael to have any inheritance from him. When I read this part, I got a little mad at God. Why would He make Hagar go back home only to get rejected and pushed out again? Did she waste those years trying to build a relationship with Sarah and Abraham only to be pushed aside? Before, she had left on her terms, but this time it was embarrassing because they rejected her.

I remember there was a guy who begged for me to go on dates with him. So after months of his repeated attempts, I finally thought, *Hey, I'll give him a chance. He is kind of cute, and he seems nice.* I did this only for him to ghost me just three days after I finally agreed I liked him. I thought, *What?! You begged for me, and now you're not interested? You don't get to ghost me when you're the one who wanted me first!*

Obviously, Hagar had it ten thousand times worse. It is embarrassing and hurtful to be rejected after trusting someone. But we've all been there. Whether we almost quit only to be fired, trusted a friend after she betrayed us only to be betrayed again, or moved back to our hometown only to be judged again, we know the feeling.

But God isn't looking for results. He's looking for you to see Him and for you to know He sees you. God desires your boldness, not success. So even when it doesn't work out, God cares for you, mourns with you, and sees that you are growing into who you are meant to be. He is faithful to fulfill His promises to you.

When Hagar was in the wilderness for the second time, she probably felt abandoned by God. She and her son were thirsty. Ishmael was crying. The angel appeared to Hagar again. He told her that God heard her cry and reminded her that Ishmael would be the father of a great nation and that God would provide. Hagar then saw water in the desert and knew that God saw her!

God was faithful to His promises.

Hagar was bold to listen. She listened when it was messy and hard. She lifted her son in response to the angel, even after being cast away. Hagar was heard and seen, and she wasn't focused on jealousy or what people would think of her. She was focused on her faithful God who saw her.

We have all felt overlooked at some point. We have all felt like we are in a desert alone. I want you to pay attention to this next part as I share with you what God sees in you.

#1 - God sees your tears.

I used to cry only in places where no one could see me, like the bathroom, bedroom, shower, and occasionally while on a walk as I avoided the world. I thought crying was showing weakness.

When I see Hagar run away and end up somewhere more dangerous, like the desert where there are wild animals and a lack of water and food, I see you and me. I see all the times we've hidden and tried to "handle" our emotions, only to end up in a worse state than before. God sees your hurt. You are never crying alone. Run to Him and to those who point you to Him, not the desert. God sees your tears. He knows your life is meant for more than your tears. He sees your tears, comforts you in your mess, protects you, and leads you to His good.

#2 - God sees your future blessings.

You may not know these blessings yet, but He sees them. God isn't held to the confines of time. He is in the past, present, and future. Your God has seen your past hurts and still sees them today. He is with you in the present, but He also sees your future blessings. Rest in the peace that your God has it all together, even when you don't. God sees, even when you feel stuck. You do not have to worry about the next chapter of your story when you know the Author.

#3 - God sees your boldness.

When Hagar spoke out to God, naming Him the "God who sees," God saw her transformation from despair to faith. He saw her transformation from looking down in exhaustion and hurt, to listening to His voice and eventually returning to those who hurt her. God called her to go back, and He saw her make the hard decision to listen to His voice more than she listened to what she wanted. God saw this in Hagar, and He sees this in you. He sees all the times you choose to speak love and not retaliate. He sees all the times you walk to your class with boldness or take care of your neighbors with eagerness. He sees your boldness and He is proud of it.

#4 - God sees your future closed doors.

Hagar returned to Sarah and Abraham, only for them to kick her out again. Why would God send her back if He knew this would happen? I think we forget that God sees the doors that will close on us. He knows the breakups we may go through and the betrayal those friends may bring. He knows our future hurts, and even though He sees this, He knows that sometimes closed doors are purposeful and produce perseverance in us. Closed doors and rejection may come multiple times and can bring us to our knees, a perfect place to pray. Isn't it comforting to know that though we will get hurt again, God's plan is bigger than the next closed door?

#5 - God sees you for who you are.

You can run and hide, but God sees you and calls you by name. God audibly called Hagar by name when He was talking to her in the desert, which was rare for Hagar. He saw her as more than just her standing in society. He saw her for her unique soul, knitted together in her mother's womb, and called her by her name.

God sees you for your uniqueness. He doesn't care what the rumors are or how others view you. He sees you for you.

To be bold, we must know that we are seen. You may be closing this chapter while in a dorm room, in your tiny apartment, on a beach, while you wait on that guy to text you back, or while kids run around you. Maybe you're reading this chapter in the hardest season of your life. I hope you will remember how God saw Hagar and was faithful to her and know that God sees you and will be faithful to you too.

PART 4

What Will They Think If I Obey God?

"I am the Lord's servant," Mary answered. "May your word to me be fulfilled." Then the angel left her.

LUKE 1:38

CHAPTER 7

Learn from Mary

WHAT WERE YOUR BIGGEST ASPIRATIONS AT AGE FOUR-teen? You were probably in ninth grade, doodling the initials of some boy who barely talked to you, practicing a dance in your living room (I'm now thankful that TikTok didn't exist back then), stressing over pre-algebra, listening to some dramatic song about heartbreak you'd never experienced, running to the fridge during the commercial break between *Hannah Montana* episodes, and maybe, just maybe, dreaming about making your name great. You may have been a young girl, but you probably had big dreams.

I remember being fourteen and wanting to be popular. That was my main goal. I wanted to be cool in school and, one day, be known by everyone. I remember overthinking every social outing. And there was nothing worse than feeling left out. You know that awful feeling when you realize there's a group text that doesn't include you? That sinking pit felt a hundred times worse when you were fourteen, breaking out, and mid-puberty.

I remember one time my mom dropped two friends and me off at a shopping center in my suburban town. At fourteen, this was the closest to freedom I could feel. Unfortunately, three is always a weird number for a friend group. Add the pettiness of insecure teenagers who don't know their purpose, and it gets worse. It was my idea for us to hang out. I wanted to convince them to like me, and I thought maybe we would try on bras too big for us, giggle, and end up as besties. Maybe while squeez-ing into jeggings at American Eagle, they would look over at me and invite me to the exclusive sleepover I knew they had every weekend. But as we shopped they seemed to hang out more with each other than with me. I would try to talk, but someone's voice would overpower mine. I would share a funny joke and feel the awkward silence. I would watch them share similarities while I sat there confused about what they were talking about.

Remember that sinking pit? I felt it that day. I kept trying to contribute to the conversation but was denied.

Then we went to Victoria's Secret. Although I wasn't as developed as they were at the time, of course I wanted a glittery white snap-in-the-front bra like the other girls were getting. While we were there, one of the girls, we'll call her Ashley, reached over my shoulder and asked me a question in a mean tone: "Grace! Why are you breathing that loud?! It is not fun to be with someone who breathes like *this* . . ." Then she did a loud panting while giggling. The other girl laughed too. I teared up. Then I was scared of even breathing. *Is it too loud? Am I weird? Can they see me cry?*

How dare I *breathe*.

Mean girl Ashley saw my tears and said, "OMG. Grace, it was just a joke!"

Yeah, like that made it better. My tears fell harder. I went to the bathroom and dried off my tears until someone's mom picked us up.

"Did y'all have fun, girls?" she asked us.

"Yes!" we said in unison.

Of course, I was the first to be dropped off at home. And yes, the two of them did hang out after that without me. I was apparently this pathetic mouth-breather who felt left out this whole day, but supposedly it was okay because "it was just a joke."

I wonder how Ashley is doing today. I realize now that chances are she was just like me, also insecure and trying to be seen as cool, but her solution was simply to belittle me, the weak link. All I wanted was a snap-in-the-front bra and two friends who liked me—was that too much to ask for?

The truth is, we all probably struggled in ninth grade. We felt insecure. Sadly, we don't grow out of insecurity; we just present it differently. Maybe it is yelling at a girl for breathing loud at fourteen, but then one day it is yelling at strangers on the internet. One day it is tearing someone apart in the name of sorority recruitment. The next it is being a mom who gossips about younger girls in high school. And suddenly we're talking smack in the nursing home.

Insecurity is normal and a part of this sinful world. But maybe we struggle so much with feeling insecure because we have idolized how others view us. Yes, I cried because a fourteen-year-old said I breathed loud, but the truth is I cried mainly because I cared too much about what people thought.

I can list millions of times I've cried in bathrooms. I've locked myself behind closed doors to wallow in my tears, let my mascara run, and feel pathetic. From boys, to mean girls, to feeling left out, to a toxic work environment, to family drama, and so much more. But sometimes I look back and remember all the tears I cried about how someone viewed me, and I get frustrated. What a poor excuse for tears. I couldn't control their opinion, and even worse, I was distracted and missing out on my true purpose.

I bet you, too, can list many of the stupid things you've cried about, especially when you were fourteen years old. From loud breathing, to chubby fingers, to feeling like the third wheel. Maybe you got on Snapchat and saw everyone hanging out without you, or maybe you found out there's a group text that doesn't include you. Perhaps you cried because you realized they thought about you less or lower than you wished.

But let's look at Mary. At fourteen years old, I was overthinking my breathing patterns because Ashley wanted to be top dog. Mary was being approached by an angel.

As was common in their culture, Mary was about fourteen when she was engaged to marry Joseph. And then an angel approached her, saying, "Greetings, you who are highly favored! The Lord is with you" (Luke 1:28). Verse 29 describes Mary's response to this angelic announcement: "She was startled by what the angel said and tried to figure out what this greeting meant" (GW). Although Mary was startled at first, I think it is inspiring that instead of doubting that God or the angel that approached her was even real, she tried to figure out what the greeting meant. She was focused on understanding God's will, not questioning His existence.

When we look at other stories in the Bible—such as the one in Matthew 14:22–33 where Jesus was walking on the water during the storm—many times His disciples thought Jesus was a ghost, not God at work. When we read other stories of people who encountered God, we often see them run away. But Mary sat there and tried to figure it out. She probably was more attentive than I am at 9:00 a.m. meetings, and she listened eagerly to what God had in store for her. Being startled doesn't mean you're afraid; it just means you're surprised. It means you weren't expecting something to happen. I think you and I both have many moments in our everyday lives that startle us. It could be bad news, crazy news, a breakup, a promotion, a pregnancy, or other unexpected things we have to deal with. Maybe we should learn from Mary and handle startling news the way she did.

The angel continued to tell Mary that she would have a child and this child would be conceived by the Holy Spirit. He didn't give her much detail, just these words: "The Holy Spirit will come to you, and the power of the Most High will overshadow you. Therefore, the holy child developing inside you will be called the Son of God. Elizabeth, your relative, is six months pregnant with a son in her old age. People said she couldn't have a child. But nothing is impossible for God" (Luke 1:35–37 GW).

It's often easy to think, *God isn't giving me enough detail to help me trust Him.* When I was furloughed, I was angry because I felt God telling me, *I'm leading you to more peace.* But my bills were piling up, I was stressed, and I wished He would make His plan a little clearer. Before I go on first dates, I think of the "Blank Space" Taylor Swift lyric, "It's gonna be forever, or it's gonna go down in flames," because the truth is I never know how it will end. He could break my heart, ghost me, annoy me, or be the love of my life. I wonder why God can't just flash a green light from above and say, *This is a good one, Grace!*

Imagine how you would feel if you were Mary. You're excited to get married and start a life with Joseph, and you've never had sex. Then all of a sudden, an angel comes to you and basically says, "Hey, don't be afraid. You're going to be pregnant by the Holy Spirit . . . oh, and this child is going to be the Savior of the world. See ya in nine months!"

Mary's response to the angel seems crazy to me. After hearing this news, she said, "I am the Lord's servant. Let everything you've said happen to me" (Luke 1:38 GW).

Incredible! Let's break down her response, because I believe it can teach us a lot.

"I am the Lord's servant."

I often refer to myself as a child of God, beloved, forgiven, enough, and a vessel for God. Those things are true, but if you're anything like me, you'd agree that it isn't as fun to call yourself a servant of God. See, I want to serve my dreams, my desire to be popular and rich, my desire to have a Christian family one day, and my desire to be a boss others look at and think, *Dang, she has her life together.*

In a world where everyone wants to be the main character, I pray we can be like Mary and know our role. In a world that tells us to chase our dreams and be big, I hope we can be content to sit at the feet of our big God. And on the days we want to serve our fleshly desire to be liked, to prove ourselves, and to be successful, I hope we can remember our true purpose comes from being the Lord's servant.

"Let everything you've said happen to me."

If there's one thing that scares me, it is praying to the Lord, "Let Your will be done." I want *my* will to be done. I want a cute Christian guy to meet me in a Trader Joe's aisle when I least expect it, since that seems to be where all the Christian girls meet their husbands. Oftentimes, my prayers are selfish (I'm working on it, I promise) and about things I want. When I was in ninth grade—that awkward fourteen-year-old—I remember praying to be popular. I've prayed for good friendships in my twenties and a job that *I* wanted, not one that the Lord wanted for me. I've prayed about my wants and desires. I've made my prayers about myself. There is nothing wrong with giving God your wants, but are you giving God your life? If Mary could give her body to carry our Savior, then let that challenge and encourage us to give Jesus our all.

Mary heard everything the angel said would happen, realized everything the angel didn't say would happen, and prayed for it to happen, which reveals her amazing faith. That might have sounded like a tongue twister, but stick with me. I think it is incredible that Mary said what she did after the angel gave her four sentences, if even that. Do you know what Mary didn't hear? Here are some things the angel did *not* say to Mary:

I know you're engaged and being pregnant outside of wedlock could threaten your life, but you'll be okay, I promise.

It might be hard at first, but there's a light at the end of it all. Push forward.

So you're not going to conceive a child with a man; you're actually using this cool tool called the Holy Spirit. Here's how this will play out and the research to prove you and your baby will be healthy!

Mary wasn't given a motivational pep talk by the angel or promised that she would be safe. The angel didn't promise her popularity. He just said this was the Lord's will and not to be afraid, and Mary was content with that. She didn't search for more clarity or wait for another sign from God. She focused fully on obeying her calling.

If it were you or me, chances are we would've liked the angel to have given us more details. And I bet Mary wanted that, too, but she trusted God. She knew her purpose wasn't to stop the small-town gossip, or to be likeable to her own fiancé, but to live out God's will.

I wonder what crazy things we could do if we learned from Mary. If we truly want to find purpose and be bold in this world, we need to learn several things.

You can be startled but be ready.

God may reveal something to you tonight, tomorrow, next week, or four years from now. Pray for Him to reveal His will for you. Pray for even your dreams to be tools for this; yes, God can still speak to us in dreams. But always remind yourself to be like Mary and to consider what God's doing and saying instead of trying to decide if He even exists. Mary never doubted it was God. She was focused on discerning what His will was. Maybe boldness starts with enough faith to believe God is there, revealing things to us in the moments we least expect it.

Know your role.

We are not meant to be main characters or the stars of the show. We are called to serve God. Humble yourself and sit at Jesus' feet. Listen to Him more than you try to ask from Him. God won't be able to talk to you if you're too busy using your prayer time asking for more and more worldly things. I hope you get your dream career, work hard, kill it at that Wednesday meeting, do some squats, join all the clubs, and make great friends, but I hope even more that you serve your God more than you serve your dreams. Let's not live in a way that, if Jesus came back and all this was over and we were in heaven, we would be sad that we didn't get the cute marriage, precious children, perfect job, or other worldly dreams.

Pray for crazy to happen.

I pray for safety more than I pray for God's will to be done—and that needs to change. The boldest thing we can do is to simply pray for God's will to be done not just *for* us but *through* us. Pray to have a hand in the craziest love story of all time. I want our responses to be crazy; to be like Mary's. Mary immediately prayed for His will to be done instead of panicking about whether she was qualified, or if her fiancé would leave her, or if she would be socially excluded or even killed. We have to remember that, back then, Mary wasn't just risking some harsh gossip about her. Women who were believed to have cheated on their fiancés or husbands, or women who got pregnant before marriage, were often stoned. This wasn't just a moral no-no; it was often against the law. Mary knew this yet still responded with eagerness to obey.

Be okay with not knowing all the details.

Mary didn't have details, but she did have her big God. You may feel a deep calling in your heart right now; however, you want

God to give you a five-year plan, all the details, and promises that you'll be safe, well-liked, and successful. But being bold isn't about being safe. And being bold isn't about knowing how it gets done. It is about knowing why it needs to be done. Know your why. When you know that your life is about being love in a world that doesn't know the Author of love, it is easier to walk boldly. When you realize that each day God gives you is an opportunity to share the name of the One who died for you, loves you more than you deserve, and cares for you, it is easier to be bold. You may not know how, but you can still give it to God. If He has called you to it, then He'll make a way for you. Be bold enough to know you don't need details; you just need your faithful God. He is faithful to His promises, and His will is greater than any worldly desire.

If I could go back to my fourteen-year-old self, the loud-breathing outcast, I would tell her, "You'll meet Ashleys in all seasons." (Seriously, I'm so sorry if this is actually your name. I don't mean literal Ashleys, just mean people.) "You'll meet plenty of people who don't think fondly of you and plenty of people who try to put you down for their own gain."

I would also tell my fourteen-year-old self this:

Hey, Grace. It is hard. You're allowed to cry. Crying isn't a sin, and the rejection you're facing is real. The sinking pit you feel when hurt and left out is your worldly body craving something this world can never provide. I know you desperately want to fit in, be liked, make a name for yourself, and convince the Ashleys to like you. But you weren't called to be liked, and you'll do much bigger things than sit at that one lunch table. Mary was a woman in the Bible who didn't try to be liked, popular, or the main character. She just chose to be a servant of God. If you want to do big things, you need to know and trust your big God. Not everyone will like you, but your purpose isn't to prove yourself. You're not a restaurant waiting on a Yelp review or a product to be enjoyed. You're a servant and daughter of Christ. Choose boldness over being liked.

And to you, whether you're in your teens, twenties, thirties, or wherever you are right now, I pray whenever you encounter an Ashley, you look up. Thank goodness your role isn't to be Ashley's bestie or to be everyone's favorite main character in a romantic comedy. We are called to serve a mission greater than the one others set out for us. May we do big things with our big boldness because we know and trust in our big God.

CHAPTER 8

Five Things
Mary Wasn't
Worried About

ONE OF MY FRIENDS WAS THROWING A BACHELORETTE party in Nashville, and it was my first time in a big city like this. Usually, my friends had bachelorette parties that were chill weekends with fun and intimate time with their friends. But my friend Abbie Joe wanted to go all out in the city known for being the best place to have a bachelorette party. I remember thinking, *Finally, it's my chance to look cute in Nashville and maybe bump into a famous yet available country music star while I'm dancing with my girls.* Even though the weekend was going to be about my friend Abbie Joe, I couldn't wait to experience the bright lights of Music City.

What you should know is that most bachelorette parties have dress codes. Some make the girls wear cute black outfits, and the bride wears white. One bachelorette party I went to had us wear hot pink outfits, and the bride wore white. But I'll never forget Abbie Joe giving our instructions on what to wear:

She was having a "Joe theme" night.

I know what you're thinking: *What is a "Joe theme"?* I was confused too. Basically, we were required to dress up as different places, people, or things with the word *Joe* in it.

Someone dressed like a crab because she was Joe's Crab Shack.

Someone dressed like everyone's favorite teenage dancer, JoJo Siwa.

Someone dressed as Trader Joe's, my favorite grocery store.

Someone dressed as Joe Rogan . . . I don't need to go on about that.

And you know what my friend Abbie Joe had me dress up as? Joe Jonas. Let me be honest with you: I love Joe Jonas. He's been my favorite pop star since the Disney movie *Camp Rock* aired. I'm pretty sure I figured out what hormones were when Joe Jonas starred on *Hannah Montana*. I'd admire his long and straightened brown hair while he sang about saving the environment during my commercials between Disney episodes, and it made me believe in love at that young age (joking but not). But here I was in Nashville, in a city with music celebrities and cute country boys, dressed like the emo Jonas we all knew in 2009. I was wearing a short brunette wig and leather pants with, of course, a thin red scarf.

I thought, *No way I'll kiss a country star in a Broadway bar tonight. Bummer.*

Just kidding. We can all agree that I wouldn't even come close to kissing a boy in a bar because #standards. But now that I was dressed like Joe Jonas and not some cute bachelorette attendee in a black minidress, that solidified my destiny of being kissless and not being hit on; I could instead focus on my favorite Joe—my friend Abbie Joe.

I ended up having a great time dressed as Joe Jonas. I got more compliments than I ever did when I tried to look hot. And I had more fun! I had more fun when I was dressed like Joe Jonas because my purpose was no longer to be hot, convince a guy I was worthy of his attention, or to be the main character. I danced like a fool, and guess what? Some guy asked for my number . . . while I was wearing a wig, leather pants, and Converse.

In the past, on rare occasions with friends when I did go out to socialize casually, I was so consumed with what others thought of me:

Does this dress make me look fat?

Does this color wash me out?

Should I dance, or should I sit down and look available for a guy to come up to me?

Should I go out even if I don't want to because I feel like that's the only way to make friends or find love?

It's funny because we all do it. I remember hearing that a major TikTok star and model read my first book on insecurity, and she posted about it on her TikTok. After she posted it, we got connected, and she told me that she took my book with her to her modeling shoots around the world. So even though she was famous for being beautiful and her career was focused around physical beauty, she still had insecurities. She had long legs, probably was a size 0, yet still felt insecure. What the heck?

I used to work at a Christian camp, and we used to have a night with the boys called Midnight Skating, when we would take our campers to a roller rink and boys from an all-boys camp would meet us there. Before it was time to get ready, the girls would have some free time. During that time, the other camp counselors and I would jump in the pool or lake, hang out with friends, and have fun. But the campers would start preparing for Midnight Skating even before dinner. They would stare in the mirror for hours, adding one more layer of makeup, switching their earrings five times, and overthinking their outfits. I would do my best to encourage these young girls not to get ready so early because if you stare in the mirror for hours, you're going to get insecure.

We've all been there. That sinking pit of insecurity. That late-night drive to the gym trying to force your body to look like what you think others want. Let me remind you that working out should never be a punishment for what you ate or what you look like. Working out should always be a celebration of what your body can do, not a punishment for what you have done. I hate that so many of us have unhealthy relationships with our bodies, but I believe the Enemy does this on purpose. He desires for you to make your body an idol, and he slithers into your thoughts hoping you care more and more about what your body looks like, and in return, you ignore the beauty and the truth that comes from knowing what your body can do.

I want us to look at Mary, the mother of Jesus, and see several things she wasn't worried about. In a world where we believe our lives are about our dreams and pleasing others, and that our bodies are résumés of our worth, it is comforting to see that Mary wasn't worried about these five things.

#1 - Mary wasn't worried about her love life.

Let's be real. If you're anything like me, my friends, or my friends' friends, whether single, dating, engaged, married, or divorced, it is easy to overthink your love life. I remember after my first book came out, someone who used to be a mentor in my life said something I disagreed with. She looked me in the eye and said, "It is great you published one book, but maybe that needs to be it."

I was confused. God called me to write. I knew He wanted me to write silly stories of mine and write easy-to-understand explanations about His Word. So I asked her to explain, and here's what she said:

"Well, it is awesome what you're doing; it really is . . . but this is going to turn away a guy. He'll think you're more successful or know God's Word more than he does, or you'll be too honest about your life and he won't want to marry you. You should put your writing on hold until after you have a husband, and then you can ask his permission."

I disagreed with so many points in her statement. I hope I meet a man one day, but I hope I meet a holy man. I hope I meet a man who, like Mary's husband, Joseph, can hear God's plans himself. I hope he supports me in my crazy, and I hope I push him to be bold.

The Bible indicates that, at first, Joseph thought Mary cheated on him when she became pregnant. Well, that's understandable. Joseph knew he hadn't slept with Mary, so how else would she have become pregnant?

We don't know if Mary was crying every night, praying Joseph wouldn't leave her. We don't know if she was begging him to believe her. We do know Joseph was preparing to separate from her, though he was kind enough to do it privately, because back then, if a woman was even accused of cheating, she could be put to death. However, Mary's first reaction wasn't to ask God if Joseph would stick around. She was focused fully on being a servant of God. She wasn't stressing over her man. She was focused on serving her God. Granted, when you're married, two become one and you should chase God together, but you should still remember that first and foremost you are a child of God and servant of our Savior.

If you're anything like me, you know what it is like to cry because of silly boys who don't care enough. I love that the Bible gives us a picture of a godly woman like Mary and also the picture of a humble man like Joseph. He didn't get jealous that Mary was bearing the Lord's Son. He humbly celebrated Mary's unique calling, just as she celebrated his. So if you're scared your boldness will scare away a man, then you're not being bold enough. Be bold enough to realize that any man who thinks your calling is "too much" is missing out on our powerful God.

#2 - Mary wasn't worried about her body.

When Mary called herself "the Lord's servant" and prayed for God's will to be done (Luke 1:38), she wasn't worried about what her body would become. We hear people often reference the scripture that says your body is a temple of the Holy Spirit (1 Cor. 6:19). But we often forget that means our bodies aren't meant to be about us. I like working out, but this past year I've had to pray over my workouts to be about celebrating what my body can do, not hating it for what it looks like. I hope you do your squats, work out, run that mile, and eat fresh fruit, but I hope more so that you're bold enough to see that your body on this earth is simply a vessel God can use.

Look at your legs. You may see something that you complain about to your friends, and maybe you wish they were thinner, more toned, or even bigger. But your legs have carried you this far. They can walk through your campus and take you to conversations and friendships where you can spread the gospel. Your arms have hugged many friends who have cried tears over hurt, trials, breakups, and more. Your arms can reach the least of these and help others physically feel known. Your eyes can see the best in others and help the forgotten feel seen. Your mouth can speak kindness and can offer the words someone may need to carry on. Your mouth can also share the gospel and the good news of what

Jesus has done. Your body is good. There may be some of you who feel like your body has failed you because maybe you can't walk, or you lost your eyesight, or your health is failing. However, all our hearts are still pumping, and that is God whispering to each of us, saying, *Continue to be bold. I'm not finished with you yet.*

I still sometimes struggle with body image, but I found boldness in my purpose when I realized my body has a mission greater than being attractive, looking good in a dress, and being toned. My body gets to be a temporary home for my spirit and the Holy Spirit. My body is a vessel that God can use to spread the gospel. Mary knew her body was about more than even bearing children. She knew her body was not meant to be an idol, but a vessel to make God's name great. So when the angel told Mary that her body would be a crib for our Savior, she simply asked how it could happen and said let it be done.

What if we prayed to let God's will be done with our physical bodies? What if instead of looking in the mirror and speaking lies about our worth we asked God to show us what He wants to use our physical bodies for? Imagine what the Lord could do.

#3 - Mary wasn't worried about the details.

As I mentioned before, Mary got little to no information about what would happen. All she knew was God had favor on her, she was a virgin bearing a child conceived by the Holy Spirit, and this was going to be a wild ride. She trusted in God and expected His miracles to get her through the confusing parts. In a world where people doubt God because He isn't clear enough, maybe we should take some tips from Mary. She knew her role wasn't to decide what

God would do but to pray for God's will to be done. She trusted in His will and didn't ask to know all the details.

You may be reading this now, and you don't know where you'll be next year, if your current job is what you're called to do, if you'll find a spouse, if your husband will come back to you, if you'll get into a sorority, if you'll ever find true friendships, or even if you will get through this year. Whatever you're wondering about right now, it is important to remember we don't have to have the details when we have our God.

Instead of asking God for the details, let's be like Mary and ask for His will to be done.

#4 - Mary wasn't worried about missing out.

I remember being in college when God called me to remove myself from the party scene. The party scene in college tempted me to feel insecure and drink to the point of blacking out, and it was making me stressed. This was right before we had a Tuesday off school called Diadeloso, which stood for the "Day of the Bear," and even though they bring a petting zoo to campus, most Baylor students used this day to party. I was worried I would miss out on fun when I left the party scene, but I stood by what I felt like I needed to do after prayer to help my faith in that season. Instead of going out, I wrote on my blog, worked on my first book, and drove my friends who were drinking to get fast food, to their next party, and home. After Dia was over, I remember thinking, *Dang, I didn't miss anything.*

When you're boldly following God, you won't miss out. I wish someone would've told nineteen-year-old, party-scene Grace, who had a lot of hangovers and heartaches, that she didn't need to drown her personality in shots to have fun. I wish someone would've told me God's best is better than even my own expectations. But I'm glad I know it now.

You won't miss out on anything worthwhile if you choose to follow God boldly. You won't miss out on fun college nights, because you'll gain even crazier adventures when you follow Jesus. I mean, Mary was a virgin teenager bearing the Lord's Son conceived by the Holy Spirit. It doesn't get more adventurous than that!

If you choose to follow God boldly, you won't miss out on a good relationship. Mary first and foremost had a relationship with God, and even though we aren't promised a husband, in this case we can see that God did give Mary just the man she needed to humbly walk with her through her purpose. Maybe you don't have a boyfriend or even a lot of dates, but this may just be God leading you to the right one to walk with you through your purpose. You won't miss out on success when you realize your legacy in this world has nothing to do with how much money you made or how well known you are. When you walk boldly with Jesus, you'll realize that living a kind and loving life in the name of the Author of love is more powerful than any worldly success.

When we see Mary, we see someone who was focused more on being bold and trusting in God's best than worrying about missing out.

#5 - Mary wasn't worried about her age.

Mary was a young teenage girl when the angel told her she would bear God's Son, even though she was a virgin. I am amazed that in her response she didn't protest that she was too young. We live in a world that teaches students and high schoolers to prepare for "one day." I remember being told to take AP classes in high school to prepare me for college. I remember being told to take a career quiz to help me prepare for life after college. I remember being told to join this club, do this activity, work this job, and rearrange a lot of my time in the present to prepare for my future.

There is nothing wrong with telling teenagers they should take an AP test or do some résumé boosters, but I do believe there is something wrong with *always* working hard for the future. Imagine all the opportunities we would miss out on today if we focused only on our future. If you're so worried about your future that you don't ask your neighbor about his life, you may never know his dad died last week. If you're focused on your promotion instead of your brother, you may miss out on having him over for dinner and spending time together. And if Mary had focused on preparing for how God would use her someday in the future, she may have missed out on God using her at her current age.

You are not too young, and you are not too old. Purpose isn't an exclusive right you get once you get a big-girl job, and just because you have gray hair doesn't mean you've retired from God's purpose. Mary focused on what the angel said was God's will, not the benchmarks she thought were supposed to happen for her at each age. God's blessings and callings are good, but they often come when you least expect them. They may come tomorrow, and you may have another call from God when you're sixty-seven. Focus on listening to God now more than you focus on preparing for someday. Your purpose isn't what will happen or what has already happened; your purpose is what you're living today. Expect God to use you, and don't be worried about your age.

Here's the truth: I hope you have crazy adventures, you embrace your every day, and you find joy in the little moments of life. But mainly I pray and hope you'll be like Mary. I pray you'll walk in boldness and realize your body is a vessel for God. I pray when life feels confusing and you don't have all the details, you'll walk into the unknown, confident that your God knows you and is leading you to His will. I pray you will ask for God's will to be done more than you worry about missing out.

And I hope on the days when we are looking in our closet wondering, *What should I wear today?* we won't pick the outfit we think will give us attention. I pray that all our decisions—from what we wear, to how we talk about our bodies, to the places we choose to work, to the people we do life with—will be about serving the Lord. May we pray for the Lord's will to be done and be the kind of women who are adventurous enough to serve the Lord whenever we are called.

PART 5

What Will They Think If I'm an Outcast?

Many of the Samaritans from that town believed in him because of the woman's testimony, "He told me everything I ever did."

JOHN 4:39

CHAPTER 9

Learn from the Woman at the Well

SHAME IS AN UGLY THING. IT CAN CAPTURE YOUR thoughts and make you believe lies:

I must hide from others because of who I am.

I don't deserve this kind of love because I've done this.

This whole "being loved by God" thing is cool, but it's not for someone with my kind of past.

Shame highlights what we have done and, in return, makes us forget what Jesus has done. Shame often gets mistaken for conviction, but they are two very different things. Shame makes us feel like we need to hide, while conviction makes us feel like we need to change. Shame makes us feel worthless, while conviction reminds us of who is worthy.

When I was at Baylor, it was no secret I was a little wild. I remember someone brought this sweet, innocent girl to a party my sophomore year. I was throwing back shots, and seeing the way I pounded the alcohol made her cry. Sweet little Beth Anne (not her actual name) was brought to a party her first week of college and immediately got overwhelmed by seeing me. This girl then joined my sorority and wasn't too fond of me. I'll never forget, though, when I was three years post-grad, being at a conference to help me develop my writing career, miles away from my college mistakes and miles away mentally from my wild nights. One of my friends at the conference looked at me and said, "Oh, I forgot to tell you something crazy. My current roommate is Beth Anne! She just told me she saw our picture together and knew you in college."

I thought, *Oh great. Sweet Beth Anne. She obviously hates me, and now this girl probably hates me. She probably already told my new friend about my wild nights and how I once took a pull of cheap vodka in front of everyone.*

I immediately started sweating. Now will this girl question my values because she knows this girl who remembered me when I was crazy?

I smiled and said Beth Anne was sweet, and she proceeded to insist we send her a picture. "Oh, Beth Anne will want to see this."

No, she won't, Sally. She's probably going to see me and be triggered by my nineteen-year-old, sloppy-drinking self.

She sent the picture, and I got nervous. I just knew Beth Anne was judging me. After the picture was sent, I told my new friend about how Beth Anne knew me when I was crazy, and she probably didn't have the best stories about me. I told her that I was sure she talked bad about me, but I'm not that same person anymore. My new friend looked at me and smiled sincerely. She said, "Grace, I can promise you she has only said kind things about you. She even has your book and said she was proud she knew you."

And as she told me this, her phone dinged. It was Beth Anne replying to our picture, saying, "Love this! Send Grace my love!"

Have you ever allowed shame to write lies about what others think of you and even sometimes what your God thinks of you? I allowed my own shame about my past to make me believe that Beth Anne hated me, that my new friend had heard crazy stories, and that I needed to feel awkward because of who I once was. And if I'm going to be honest, shame still sometimes causes me to believe the lie that God doesn't fully love me. Maybe you have done this too.

There are two women I want us to discuss. Two who are unique in their stories, but their lives were shaped by their relationship with their Savior. Two women who were given shame from the world, but the Lord gave them freedom. Two women others likely talked bad about, but two women who were bold enough to love Jesus despite the gossip of others.

The woman at the well felt shame because of her past and present, but her Savior gave her the conviction she needed to become new and then share her story with others.

The woman who reached for Jesus' robe had been bleeding for years and was told by her society she needed to stay put, but she boldly reached out to Jesus, was honest about her choice to reach out to Him in public, and was healed.

Both these women had people gossiping about them, assumed people hated them, and tried to avoid people—until they met Jesus and experienced freedom.

Woman at the Well

I first want to talk about the woman at the well. What is interesting is she wasn't physically healed like the other woman we will discuss. She just had an honest conversation with her good Savior. She just unexpectedly met her Savior in the middle of her mess. When no one else would want to be seen with her, her Savior said she could have eternal life. So often we let shame name us, and we allow shame to be the poison we consume. Shame becomes our name.

Maybe your shame causes you to think others are always talking about you. Maybe your shame causes you to believe the lies that others have said about you. Maybe your shame causes you to have social anxiety, because now you're so sure people are only talking about you.

The woman at the well is often talked about because of her past, but so often I think we also forget she was a Samaritan woman. Samaritans were hated by the Jewish people. These cultures did not get along due to a lengthy history of division. So this Samaritan woman had gone to get water at the well, which she chose to fetch during the hottest time of the day, around noon. Most women chose to go in the early morning or evening when the sun wasn't blazing hot. I cut my own grass (told you I was independent), and if there's one thing I've learned, it is not to cut my grass at noon in Florida. It is painful, to say the least. But this woman would rather face the heat than her peers. The well was where men would come to meet women and where women connected with other women. It was their version of a sorority and a dating app, I guess. Anyway, she wanted to avoid seeing other women and men, so she chose to fetch water in the blazing heat. But to her surprise, she wasn't alone this time.

When she arrived to draw water from the well and hopefully avoid everyone, she saw a tired Jesus sitting at Jacob's well. John 4:7–10 tells us what happened:

> Jesus said to her, "Will you give me a drink?" (His disciples had gone into the town to buy food.) The Samaritan woman said to him, "You are a Jew and I am a Samaritan woman. How can you ask me for a drink?" (For Jews do not associate with Samaritans.) Jesus answered her, "If you knew the gift of God and who it is that asks you for a drink, you would have asked him and he would have given you living water."

Here she was, avoiding the murmurs and weird looks by

coming at noon, and she was completely shocked that this Jewish man would even ask her for a drink of water. He was going against the customs for most Jewish men. But then, Jesus gave her a hint about who He was and basically said if she knew the gift of God and that He was the Son of God, she wouldn't have been afraid and would have asked Him for a drink of living water, which is salvation.

Their conversation continued:

"Sir," the woman said, "you have nothing to draw with and the well is deep. Where can you get this living water? Are you greater than our father Jacob, who gave us the well and drank from it himself, as did also his sons and his livestock?" Jesus answered, "Everyone who drinks this water will be thirsty again, but whoever drinks the water I give them will never thirst. Indeed, the water I give them will become in them a spring of water welling up to eternal life." (John 4:11–14)

This woman called out Jesus for showing up to the well without any of the supplies needed to draw the water. He didn't have the rope and the bucket or whatever they used to get the water. So how was He planning on getting her this "living water"? Was He trying to say He was more special than their ancestors who gave them this well?

Jesus responded to her in a way that

- boldly claimed He offered something greater than that which helps our physical need for thirst; and
- inspired her to boldly accept this water as the passage continues.

Let's also understand this metaphor Jesus was explaining. Wells were crucial back then, and the mere idea that Jesus was pointing to this life-changing well and saying "Hey, this well isn't enough" was Jesus showing us that the only one who can satisfy the human heart is the One who created and saved us. Water is what keeps us alive, but Jesus is what keeps our spirits alive. Wells dig deep to find the source they think will lead to water. What happens when a well is dug deep in the wrong area? They may find what looks like water and tastes like water but is a poisonous liquid that can kill them. If your water isn't clean, you can die. So many of us see things in this world that feel fun and seem to bring happiness, but really over time, like a well giving us poisonous water, they are destroying us.

John 10:10 explains that the thief, which is Satan, comes to "steal and kill and destroy." When we fall for his lies and draw our lives from a well that is focused on success, financial power, looks, being liked, or being wanted, we are slowly allowing Satan to steal, kill, and destroy not just our purpose but our lives. When we draw water from the lies of Satan and miss out on the bold life given by our Savior, we cowardly miss out on eternity in heaven and purpose in this lifetime.

So what Jesus was offering her was a big deal. But Jesus then made this offer personal.

The woman said to him, "Sir, give me this water so that I won't get thirsty and have to keep coming here to draw water." He told her, "Go, call your husband and come back." "I have no husband," she replied. Jesus said to her, "You are right when you say you have no husband. The fact is, you have had five husbands, and the man you now have is not your husband.

What you have just said is quite true." "Sir," the woman said, "I can see that you are a prophet. Our ancestors worshiped on this mountain, but you Jews claim that the place where we must worship is in Jerusalem." "Woman," Jesus replied, "believe me, a time is coming when you will worship the Father neither on this mountain nor in Jerusalem. You Samaritans worship what you do not know; we worship what we do know, for salvation is from the Jews. Yet a time is coming and has now come when the true worshipers will worship the Father in the Spirit and in truth, for they are the kind of worshipers the Father seeks. God is spirit, and his worshipers must worship in the Spirit and in truth." The woman said, "I know that Messiah" (called Christ) "is coming. When he comes, he will explain everything to us." Then Jesus declared, "I, the one speaking to you—I am he." (John 4:15–26)

The woman heard Jesus talking about this water that could satisfy her thirst, and she was not just intrigued; she was sold. She wanted this water. She was tired of drawing for water and was all for never being thirsty again.

Then Jesus asked her to go get her husband. I wonder how she felt when He asked this. She quickly replied she didn't have a husband, and Jesus basically said, "You're right, and I know the truth. You've slept with a lot of men, and the one you're with now isn't your man." This woman was avoiding the shame from her peers and now had received conviction from her Savior. Conviction and judgment aren't the same thing. Conviction helps you acknowledge your sin but see your Savior. Shame causes your heart to be stolen from grace and given to the Enemy. Shame causes you to see your sin and feel stuck in your sin.

Jesus broke a lot of barriers talking to this woman. He revealed His power to this woman. This was early on in His ministry days. This was before He fed the five thousand (John 6:1–14) and walked on water (John 6:16–21). In verse 27 of this passage, the disciples were confused about why Jesus would talk to this woman: "Just then his disciples returned and were surprised to find him talking with a woman. But no one asked, 'What do you want?' or 'Why are you talking with her?'"

No Jewish leader back then would ever be seen talking to a Samaritan woman with a bad reputation. They would shame her. She would accept the shame and never live in grace. But Jesus called her up. He didn't want her to keep participating in sexual immorality, but He wanted her to accept the living water, Himself. He wanted her to realize He, the Messiah, came for her personally. He wanted her to know that He knew her past, and guess what? Her past didn't exclude her from a future with Jesus.

Maybe in your past you've felt shame. Maybe you've slept around, found your worth in your money, chosen stress over trust, cared more about being liked than about knowing your Savior, cheated, lied, or gossiped. Jesus came for each of us. He sees our sin yet offers us a drink of living water. He knows what you did, but He also knows how much He loves you. And He wants you to boldly see Him, have an honest conversation with Him, and walk toward Him.

What happened next is the best part. This woman, who had tried to avoid others due to her shame but had now encountered her Savior, dropped her water jar to run back into town. Was she running to her Beth Anne, the girl she swore hated her? Was she running to the men who judged her? Was she running to tell all those who gossiped about her or those she was trying to avoid by getting water at noon? Scripture tells us she left her water jar and went into town, telling all about what Jesus said to her (John 4:28–29). She was bold and left shame at that well along with her jar, which was probably expensive. She left the water that wouldn't give her actual eternity and started to spread the good news.

What happened next? Her whole town believed her. Notice Scripture doesn't say she told only women. No, this woman who used to care so much about what people thought now spread the truth about Jesus to her whole town. She told them probably assuming they wouldn't listen to her because of her reputation, but they believed her. The Samaritans asked Jesus to stay longer, and Jesus said yes. These Samaritans were people looked down on by Jews, yet Jesus stayed longer with them because He knew they were loved and important. Many came to believe, but it all started when the woman at the well left her jar and left her shame (John 4:39–42).

You and I can be like this woman. Instead of assuming everyone is talking bad about us, why don't we just tell them what Jesus has done in our lives? Instead of running away from people we feel tension with, let's encounter Jesus, find true freedom and living water, and run toward them with the truth that our Savior knows us and is the Messiah. I used to think, *Man, this woman got brave—she went from running away from the town gossip to running toward it.* But the truth is, she didn't get brave; she just left the lies about her worth with that jug of water.

If we want to experience true boldness and purpose and change our cities for Jesus Christ, then we must leave our shame and burdens with Jesus. We must leave our shame after we encounter Jesus. It is easy to read this and think, *Well, I've already accepted Jesus Christ, so why do I still feel this way sometimes?* Here's my question for you: Are you having conversations with Jesus daily? Water is something we need multiple times a day, and you need conversations with the One who provides living water multiple times a day. You need Him to remind you to leave your shame and jug at the well and get to work. He makes you bold.

CHAPTER 10

Learn from the Woman Who Touched Jesus' Cloak

WHEN I HAD COVID-19 THE SUMMER OF 2020, I WAS quarantined for fourteen days. Luckily, I had two roommates at the time to make it a little less painful. But if you were quarantined for COVID, which I'm guessing most of you were, then you, too, know how lonely it can be.

During my quarantine, I turned twenty-four years old— worst birthday party ever. I also watched four seasons of *This Is Us*. So obviously, this means I cried about forty times.

I went on many walks outside and even ran in a mask. Who knows if I needed that mask since I wasn't seeing anyone, but I wasn't taking any chances of being the girl who super-spread COVID to half of Orlando.

I spent too many hours on TikTok, overthought every life choice I've ever made, and felt isolated. My lack of relationship was evident, and I wanted to be the girl quarantined with a cute husband, especially as I was scrolling through TikTok and saw what looked to be people having fun in quarantine while I was lonely, sad, and isolated. This was only fourteen days. I can't imagine being isolated longer.

But the truth is that we don't have to have a pandemic to experience loneliness and isolation. You can still feel extremely lonely even if you're never alone.

Loneliness can show up in lots of different ways:

- You're in eighth grade and get excited about being invited to the birthday party for that one girl who is kind of mean but still cool. However, you notice another girl walked in with a Vera Bradley duffel bag and quickly ran to put it in the birthday girl's room. That's when you realize you weren't invited to the VIP sleepover happening after. Snapchat confirms this happened when you're back home lying down after being too scared to talk all night at the party. Gut punch to your insecure eighth-grade self.

- Your boss calls you to the meeting with a lot of people. Everyone is throwing ideas out and you finally get the courage to speak up, but then someone talks at the same time as you. Their voice is more powerful, so everyone turns toward them. You sink in your chair and wonder if anyone even cares to hear your idea.

- Finally, you have children, something you've looked forward to forever. But then you find yourself talking in your baby voice more than your adult voice. You know all the words to every Cocomelon song and can't remember the last time you heard a DJ. You haven't gone out with lifelong friends in what seems like forever. You're so tired of changing diapers but still thankful to have a child. You feel lonely and feel like everyone has forgotten about you while you're stuck in a suburb wondering if anyone even cares.

- You go through a breakup and watch the people you thought were your friends choose to hang out with your ex, who broke your heart. You're not asking them to hate him, but you feel lonely and forgotten, while he is Mr. Perfectly Fine (yes, like the Taylor Swift song).

- It's Friday night and you're bored, so you open social media only to realize the people you thought were your closest friends are hanging out without you. You know what this means: the group text you're in with them isn't the only group text they have together. They must've created a separate group text without you. You're like that eighth grader who wasn't invited to the VIP sleepover again.

Isolation sucks. Being overlooked and forgotten sucks. We care about what people will think of us, but we also care about *if* people think of us. Sometimes they don't think to invite us, and when we get sick, no one checks in on us; they just avoid us. Sometimes our friends choose the ex, and sometimes the ex chooses the girl he told us not to worry about. We can get overlooked in meetings, and plenty of people forget our names.

When I think of the woman who touched Jesus' cloak in Luke 8, I often remember she was bleeding but forget about how isolated she was. For twelve years she was bleeding. I hate having my period for five days a month with my heavy flow—I can't imagine twelve years. When women were bleeding like this in Bible times, they were seen as ceremonially unclean. They had to be isolated socially and religiously. If she was single, she would be alone and would not get married during this time. If she was married, she would still be isolated, and her husband would have grounds for divorce since she couldn't have sex due to being unclean. This woman was trapped, alone, quarantined away from human interaction for others' supposed safety and holiness—for twelve years. Scripture tells us she had also spent all her money going to doctors searching for a cure, which only left her worse off. She was lonely, forgotten, poor, and left with no hope.

Then she heard Jesus was coming through her town. She'd

heard rumors that He could heal others. Keep in mind she probably had never seen it for herself, yet she believed in Him. She'd heard rumors of His power and what He had done, and she trusted this to be true. In her heart she had faith and believed He could heal her, even though no doctor had been able to do so. This woman chose to believe Jesus was more powerful than any doctor. So she snuck out of her isolation and entered the crowd who had isolated her and was scared of her, and in the midst of them, she waited for Jesus to pass through.

In the middle of the crowd, Scripture says, she touched the edge of Jesus' cloak and was immediately healed (Luke 8:44). Jesus noticed this, and when He asked who touched Him in verse 45, the disciples were confused by what He meant. Peter replied that multiple people had touched Him. Jesus was surrounded by a crowd of people. It was the kind of crowd like that at a sporting event or at Mardi Gras in New Orleans. Everyone leans in and brushes against you, stepping on your feet and getting in your personal space. However, in the middle of all this Jesus stopped and asked the crowd who touched Him.

In Luke 8:47, we see that the woman fell at Jesus' feet and was "trembling." She explained that she was the one who touched Him, and she did this because she believed He could heal her. When she did this, she risked punishment for not being isolated, religious judgment because the Pharisees followed strict customs and rules, and social exclusion because she went against what she was supposed to do when having these diseases. But she had risked it and now boldly fell to her knees, confessed she had touched Him, and shared she had been healed.

When I hear about this woman, here's what stands out to me:

She recognized Jesus' power.

In a world where we hate asking for help, want to do things on our own, and try to prove to others that "we got this," we need to reach out to Jesus. If you don't first trust that your Savior can defeat any pain, hurt, lie, or fear, then how can you trust that you can get through the pain, hurt, lie, or fear? If you don't first recognize that Jesus' power is big, then how can you do big things? If you don't first reach out to your big God, then how are you going to walk boldly through your big struggles?

Maybe you and I would find the courage to be bold more easily if we remembered the courage of our Savior, who went to the cross.

When filling out forms, we're often asked to include an emergency contact. For me it's either my mom or my brother. If I get married, it will be my husband. However, I think we forget that Jesus should be our emergency contact. We should have people we go to physically, but when the breakup hurts, when you think you can't stand up for yourself at work, when you're isolated and lonely, or facing any other hardship, Jesus should be the one we run to. If we truly had faith in His power to turn our trials into our testimonies and make even the hardest times into new mercies, then we would have Him as our emergency contact. Trust that His power is great enough for you to reach out to Him first.

Her faith made her a daughter of Christ.

There are only two times recorded in Scripture that Jesus called someone "daughter," so in verse 48 when Jesus looked at this woman and said, "Daughter, your faith has healed you," it's important. After her rejection and isolation, Jesus reminded her that, because of her faith, she was His. She may have lost a husband or may have been single at an age when most were married. She may have spent her days alone without Instagram or TikTok to scroll through. She was rejected and pushed aside. But Jesus called her daughter.

If you try to be bold in this world but don't know who you belong to, you're going to be bold for the wrong reasons. If you try to be bold to prove to your ex that you're a boss, to get your parents' attention, or to simply be the best, then you'll miss out on true boldness. Boldness isn't about what you do as much as why you do it. Being bold won't truly affect your community, the world, or even your life if your intention isn't to serve the One who walks boldly and consistently alongside you.

I have a friend whose dad walked out of her life and another whose dad has been distant from her since she was thirteen years old. If you can relate to that, I want you to pay attention to what I'm about to say: *Your Savior calls you daughter.* You don't just have a good Father; you have a great Father who is consistent and won't walk away. You may not have an active earthly father, but if you feel your heart pump, that is your heavenly Father saying, *I'm on this earth with you, My daughter.* You are loved, and there is no proving yourself when it comes to your true Father.

Jesus gave her the opportunity to confess her action and her belief in His power.

In the midst of a busy crowd, Jesus felt her touch. Jesus knew she touched Him, but He gave her an opportunity to confess not just to Him but to the whole crowd what she had done and why she had done it. It was bold of her to touch Him but bolder to admit to the crowd that she touched Him. She was supposed to be isolated, locked away from society, because she was ceremonially unclean. This disease likely caused her not to have many friends or intimacy in any relationship. And by confessing that she went against the custom of being isolated and entered a busy crowd, she could've been punished or even put to death for going against the rules.

But Jesus knew something was different about her touch, and He even knew who touched Him. He was 100 percent man but also 100 percent God. He felt some of His power leave His body (Luke 8:46). Even though He knew who touched Him, He purposefully gave this woman an opportunity to be bold. Jesus isn't in the business of calling others out. Jesus wasn't going to point at her and say, "Hey, I know you touched My cloak." However, though Jesus may not be in the business of calling others out, He is walking in the power to call others up. He wants to give us opportunities to rise, be bold, and speak loudly and proudly of His truth.

This woman risked her life, freedom (or what was left of it), and social and religious standing by coming to Jesus, "trembling" and admitting it was her. She was going against the customs of her society to explain what she believed Jesus could do. I think our idea of being bold is standing tall, being crazy confident in our words and posture, and having witty comebacks. However, your boldest moments will sometimes include you trembling and falling on your knees in front of your Savior. You don't need good posture to be bold or a quick comeback to be purposeful. You just need to approach your Savior with four things: honesty, humility, trust, and faith.

In your life you need to approach boldness like this. Boldness isn't prideful; it's humble. Boldness starts by going to your Savior on your knees. Boldness doesn't start with handing in your résumé or "fluffing it up" so it appears better. Boldness starts with prayer and by remembering who your God is. When you know who He is, you can remember what He can do through you.

Jesus said her faith would heal her and others.

I think we forget that our faith can make us well. Even when we are isolated, sick, hurt, forgotten, and overlooked, our God can make us well. It's important to remember that "well" doesn't mean successful, and "well" doesn't always mean physically healed like it did in this passage. "Well" means you're walking in God's best for your life.

I hope you boldly ask God for your desires. I pray you run to Him and grab the thread of His cloak. I hope you realize that, although He isn't physically passing through your time, He's beside you right now, and you can have the bold faith that reaches to Him first, even when it isn't cool and even when you're overwhelmed.

When I think of this woman, what I don't see is someone who pretended to have it all together and do something crazy on her own. I see someone who wasn't afraid to tremble and wasn't trying to save face in the moment. I see a woman who knew her Savior was powerful and trusted that touching Him was more important than following society's customs. I see a woman who didn't let the fact she was unclean stop her from going to where she felt called.

Maybe you've been taught that your emotions are dramatic or that your reputation makes you unclean, unloved, and undeserving of Jesus' grace. Maybe you struggle to take your next step and go to Jesus about your dreams, desires, and pain. But your Savior wants you, sees you, and is walking beside you right now.

I hope you have the best brunches with friends who love you despite your flaws, and I hope on the days you feel lonely, you'll be able to see the people God has given you. But most of all I pray you're bold enough to drown out the lies from the world and to touch your Savior. I pray you come to Him as you are. You don't have to be perfect, clean, the good girl, or the popular girl to be bold. You just need big faith and to believe that your God is big enough to forgive you when you repent.

In Matthew 11:28–29, Jesus said, "Come to me, all you who are weary and burdened, and I will give you rest. Take my yoke upon you and learn from me, for I am gentle and humble in heart, and you will find rest for your souls." This woman came to Jesus after rejection, hurt, abandonment, and feeling worthless to many. But she brought her burdens, hurt, and pain to Jesus and watched Him turn her mess into a miracle. I pray that in your trials you don't try to "get it together." I pray you tremble and run to your Savior.

CHAPTER 11

Five Things Better than Being Liked

A FUN FACT ABOUT ME IS THAT IN COLLEGE I WORKED for the football team as an assistant to the coaches during the week and on game day for recruiting. It was the best job ever. Also, boys always think it is cool, so that's a plus (not that I care what they think). Anyway, I felt like I was participating in a sorority rush for high school boys. College football has always excited me, but if I'm being honest, there's always one person I feel bad for: the kicker.

Maybe it's because I know what it is like to face your rival team and be dependent on a field goal with ten seconds left in the fourth quarter to break a 58–58 tie (Baylor versus TCU in 2014, if you were wondering). Maybe it's because I watched Texas A&M versus Alabama in 2021 and saw that field goal surprise all of ESPN and even the Aggie fans. But I've also watched plenty of games where the kicker missed and the game was lost. Instead of blaming the whole team, people usually blame the kicker. And then middle-aged men yell at a twenty-year-old college kid because of a football game. I want to scream, "Give him a break! He is worrying about his English lecture class, his girlfriend who sometimes goes to fraternity parties without him, and helping the team win. He's just a kid."

I feel bad for the kickers because of the pressure they must feel when the game is on the line. Yes, they have only one job, but their job has changed the game plenty of times. And if they don't get it, I fear for their direct messages and the hate that will come from people of all ages who couldn't kick a ball if they tried.

Maybe I feel so bad for these kickers because I fear disappointing people and being disliked. What's normal for them is my fear: a bunch of people watching me potentially fail and then reminding me about this failure for years to come.

I hate being disliked.

There was once this girl in college who just didn't like me. The worst part is there was no real reason other than she didn't like my personality. I wish I could say, *Well, there was one time I kissed her ex-boyfriend.* Or *Well, we did a group project, and we fought about the topic.* But nope. I did nothing to her other than bother her with my presence and personality. This girl just didn't like me for being me. I tried to find out if there was anything I could do to fix it, and I had a friend who knew her say, "I just don't think your personalities mesh well!"

I started wondering if my personality was too much. If Sally didn't like me because of my personality, then surely others thought I was too much, not enough, or annoying. I tried to change who I was to please this girl who didn't like me, but then my friends were annoyed that I was not being authentic. They preferred the real me, not the me desperately trying to be liked.

When I spent my days cowardly trying to re-create my uniqueness that God purposefully designed, I missed out. I missed out on true relationships and true boldness. I missed out on unexpected adventures that come from walking boldly in my uniqueness. I missed out.

I've never been the kicker in a tied football game trying to score the game-winning point. But I have been a girl just trying to fit in with a world I wasn't meant to fit in with. I've been the girl rejected by the cool group and the girl hated for talking too much. I've been the girl who had a nasty rumor started about her by middle-aged women, and I've been the girl left crying in a bathroom because the guy just didn't like me enough. I've cried over a boss I was never enough for and a world I didn't fit into.

I don't think when God created you and me He was trying to create a missing puzzle piece for this world. I think He created each of us uniquely. Together we are good and work for the kingdom, but we are not like a puzzle that you slam certain pieces in to fit. He created us more like origami. Some of us crease here, and each of our parts is different, but together we create something beautiful. Our pieces won't always "mesh" well, but they weren't created to mesh well. They were created to work together. There is even a passage in 1 Corinthians 12:12–27 where the author, Paul, compared the body of Christ to a human body. We all have unique personalities, personal callings, and unique gifts. When we come together, we can work together for a singular purpose.

But instead of trying to fit your personality and calling into what others like or want from you, focus on folding yourself in obedience and being who God called you to be. Your little quirks and unique details create a beautiful masterpiece. What feel like flops in your personality actually make a lovely origami creation. It would be such a shame if we stood before God and said we fit in, only to hear Him say, *That was never your purpose, My child.* When we get to heaven, it won't matter if we lost the game-winning point, didn't get leadership for our sororities, had a girl hate us, or had moms gossip about our breakups. What will matter is that we boldly stepped into our purpose and left the desire to fit in with society. What will matter is that we knew Jesus for who He is, a Savior who died on a tree for us, who although perfect and blameless took the punishment we deserve so we could have an opportunity to know God. I used to be confused about why we needed a Savior, but our God is perfect and there needed to be a bridge for us to connect with Him. Jesus was this bridge for us, because even though He was 100 percent man and walked this earth experiencing rejection, hurt, and even tiredness, He was also 100 percent God and was perfect, pure, and sinless. I hope you understand how much Christ loves you. He loves you enough to die for you, and when you confess that He is Lord, He lives in your heart forever. Accepting Christ gives you living water. Your purpose isn't just to share this living water; it is to drink and remind yourself who the living water is daily. Your Savior is yours, and He loves when you talk to Him and confess His name.

When I see the woman at the well and the woman who touched Jesus' cloak, I see two women who did just that. One was spiritually distant, sexually sinful, felt judged, and purposefully hid while living in sin. People probably called her names, and she felt stuck in this bad reputation the world had given her. In the passage, she started off hidden from society. When I was in college and people called me crazy for partying, I remember feeling stuck. There came a time when I was tired of partying, but I avoided church because that's where the people who talked bad about me were. Just like the woman at the well who avoided going there during the cooler hours, I was avoiding the gossipers.

That woman who touched Jesus' cloak was slightly different. She was viewed unclean for something out of her control. She couldn't help the rumors that were started about her. Her isolation was out of her control. She wasn't purposefully avoiding everyone. She had no choice, or she would be punished. Some of you reading this may have people who talk about you for things you can't help. You may be forced to be isolated in your new city for circumstances beyond your control.

But both these women were isolated, gossiped about, and stuck where they were. Many of us feel stuck in our people-pleasing desire. Many of us are stuck thinking *What will they think?* instead of *What does God want from me?*

The woman who touched Jesus' cloak did not doubt God's power. She risked a lot by going to the crowd following Jesus, because she went against society's rules for her. The woman at the well was bold for engaging in conversation with Jesus and, despite her past and His knowing her secret sins, listening to what He had to say and going to Jesus as she was. But both were even unique for what they did next; their initial boldness led to something even better—faithfulness. The woman who touched Jesus' cloak was bolder for confessing she touched Jesus' cloak, and the woman at the well was faithful for sharing her testimony, including her past sins, to her whole town. But these public declarations of how unclean they were before Jesus and His ability to know them and give them living water showed how strongly they believed in God's power. Both these moments show us how much God did through them. These acts were faithful and pointed to the glory of God. And in all these moments, they chose to care more about God's power and their faith in Him than they cared about being liked.

So, for you and me, let's be like these women and consider five things I'd rather be than liked:

#1 - Both women were fearless in their approach to Jesus and what they did after encountering Jesus. They risked the world's opinions through their faithfulness.

I would rather live a life that is fearless. My life should be so focused on being bold and living out my calling that when I hear someone doesn't like me or that someone wants to oppose me, I shrug it off. I should fear God and be aware of His power more than I fear the opinions of some random girl online.

> Whatever happens, conduct yourselves in a manner worthy of the gospel of Christ. Then, whether I come and see you or only hear about you in my absence, I will know that you stand firm in the one Spirit, striving together as one for the faith of the gospel without being frightened in any way by those who oppose you. This is a sign to them that they will be destroyed, but that you will be saved—and that by God. For it has been granted to you on behalf of Christ not only to believe in him, but also to suffer for him, since you are going through the same struggle you saw I had, and now hear that I still have. (Phil. 1:27–30)

Paul was writing this letter to a church while he was in prison for sharing the gospel. Keep in mind that Paul was the same person as Saul, who killed Christians, but then he heard Christ, was blinded by Christ, and served Christ to the point where he was persecuted for spreading the gospel. He reminded this church to make sure their lives represented the gospel and to "stand firm in the one Spirit" (v. 27). He reminded the church that those who opposed the gospel would one day be destroyed, but since they (the church) were standing firm in Christ, they would be saved by God. He told them not to be "frightened" in any way (v. 28).

I pray you and I will not be frightened by the thought that not everyone will like us. I pray our lives will be about standing firm and not fitting in. When you know the gospel, you live in a relationship with Jesus. May we stand firm and not be frightened.

#2 - Both these women's trials were unique, but their stories didn't define them. They ran to their Savior.

Each of these women carried their own unique trials. They had many years of rejection and many years of loneliness. The woman at the well avoided seeing people at the well by drawing water at the hottest time of the day. The woman who touched Jesus' cloak was outcast and spent all her money on trying to get well so she could one day associate with others again. Their problems were unique, their stories were unique, their conversations with Jesus were unique, but their Savior was the same. His power was the same. And this power and their faithfulness changed not only their lives but the lives of others.

I would rather be unique than be liked. Our stories are unique. Our pasts are unique. Our circumstances are unique. The woman at the well wanted to hide from her past that made her feel dirty, but when she met Jesus, she told the town about the man who called her up and out of her sinful past. The woman who touched Jesus' cloak was dealing with a rare disease she was shamed for. Publicly, she was able to highlight to others how Jesus healed her.

Your unique story and personality have the power to tell the gospel. And for all my introverts, boldness doesn't mean loudness.

Boldness is about confidently sharing truth, not loudly sharing yourself. You can be uniquely bold and introverted. And for my extroverts, being bold is about being heard, and you're not heard simply by being loud. Being bold can be loud but still gentle.

I bet you and I could convince our campuses, our small but gossipy towns, our big cities, or our jobs to like us. But then, what if we are chasing approval more than Jesus and our quest becomes about being liked? Paul wrote the book of Philippians while he was in jail for telling others about Christ. One verse that sticks out to me is Philippians 3:14: "I press on toward the goal to win the prize for which God has called me heavenward in Christ Jesus."

Paul wasn't worried about fitting in and being liked. I mean, he was in prison for the gospel he strongly believed, a gospel he used to think was false. Paul went from murdering Christians to writing a lot of the New Testament and talking about "pressing on" while in jail for spreading the gospel he once rejected. When Paul told us to press on after being punished for believing the gospel, he was telling us that our goal is Christ. We should press on toward knowing God and living for Him and should be expectant of eternity with Him. Paul chose boldness and his uniqueness over being liked.

#3 - Both these women carried their faith with confidence.

The woman at the well was confident after her encounter with Jesus and was faithful to the message He gave her. The woman who touched Jesus' cloak was confident in Jesus' power to heal her.

We, too, should carry confidence in our faith instead of wasting time trying to be liked. Notice I didn't say to be confident in your hustle, intelligence, looks, or in yourself. Be confident in your real assignment while on this earth. There will always be someone prettier than you and someone who hustles harder than you. But your purpose is to love Jesus and love others. If you know your big God and big Savior, you can do big things. But these big things aren't "main character" things. These big things aren't getting the guy at the end of the movie, and they don't always mean you become the CEO or sorority president. But these big things are purposeful things. These big things are holy things.

Holy things can look like using a late-night study session with a peer in your class to also ask her how she's doing. This conversation may start about school, but it may get deeper as she shares about past hurts and anxious thoughts. This could be the perfect time to share with her about your Savior. Holy things can be going to a meeting and choosing kindness when someone else drops the ball on an assignment. Holy things are sometimes even your private moments with Jesus when you're reading Scripture and writing your prayers. No one will see this but Jesus. And that's holy. When you are confidently remembering to live out love and know the Author of love deeply, you can leave a legacy that is greater than being a "girl with good hair" or a "girl who was well-liked." Don't get me wrong—it isn't wrong to get good positions, work hard, and sometimes just study with a peer without bringing up Jesus. But when you leave this life, your love will be your legacy. Confidently live out love. Love your Savior and love others. This is a big thing.

Both these women left with confidence to share what Jesus

had done for them. One shared in front of Jesus, and one left the ground where she was changed and walked back to the town that shamed her to tell others. Some of you may do big things the minute you meet Jesus, and some of you may have to take a walk to go where God is calling you. Be confident enough to speak up and take the steps needed.

Paul also wrote this while in prison: "Do everything without grumbling or arguing, so that you may become blameless and pure, 'children of God without fault in a warped and crooked generation.' Then you will shine among them like stars in the sky as you hold firmly to the word of life. And then I will be able to boast on the day of Christ that I did not run or labor in vain" (Phil. 2:14–16).

When you're confident in your purpose, you may have hard days and tests, but you walk in your every day without grumbling or arguing. You won't pick a fight with the bad driver on the way to work if you know your purpose is to love Jesus and use your job as a vessel to help others know Him.

I still work as a nanny to help pay my bills. Many people tell me they want to be an author and lead a ministry, but in order to financially sustain myself and this calling, I have three jobs. It gets to be a lot, and I've had to learn how to rest. But I also must have confidence in my purpose. When I feel a lack of purpose while wiping babies' butts and clocking in for my other job in the early mornings, I remind myself of and pray for confidence in my purpose.

Purpose isn't just your big dream, and you don't only need to be bold about where you want to be one day. You need to choose boldness on the early Tuesday mornings when you have that class with that strict professor and when you're driving to the job that overwhelms you. Don't grumble; stay humble. Be humble and confident in God's ability to make every day purposeful. You're not looking for a "main character" life; you're confident in His ability to give you a purposeful life today.

#4 - The women shined their light. Even though their pasts were dark, they realized the light came not from not who they were but from who God is.

I used to dream of having a spotlight on me. Maybe I just watched too many Disney Channel shows where a talent scout overheard a girl sing at the grocery store and *bam*, she became a pop star overnight. Y'all, I used to dance for the patients in the nursing home where my great-grandmother lived. These dances weren't even planned; I legitimately just jumped around. I would always ask to go to my grandmother's house so we could go to my great-grandmother's nursing home and I could put on my show.

It is normal to want attention; we truly just want to be seen and liked. As I got older, it was no longer just me wanting the attention at the nursing home; it was me wanting attention from frat guys, mean-but-cool girls, and coworkers. We fight for approval, and we want to be seen and adored, but maybe instead we should focus on shining for Jesus. When we shine Jesus' light, we care more about being a lamp that leads to Jesus and less about having the spotlight shined on us.

When I think of the woman at the well, I see someone who shined the light of Jesus. Did she have it all together? No. Had she had a few nights she regretted? Probably. But she didn't need to shine her own light; she shined the light of Jesus.

The woman who touched Jesus' cloak first tried to remain hidden. I don't think she wanted to be a light; she wanted first to touch Jesus and be one with the crowd and not be seen. But when Jesus asked who faithfully touched His cloak, she confessed. She showed the world the faithfulness she carried by touching Jesus' robe and believing in His power.

And then there's you, someone reading this with a light ready to be shared. Whether you're too scared to shine because the crowd is comforting, or you think your past makes it hard to shine, remember this light isn't dependent on who you are; it is dependent on who God is. This light will be bright not because you're worthy of shining but because God is powerful enough to use broken vessels like you and me for His glory.

Having a good attitude is the easiest way to shine your light. Do you know how many people with bad attitudes we encounter every day? Just go down your local interstate and interact with the fellow drivers. Walk the halls and listen to the conversations at the nearest high school. Be bold enough to see the good even in the hard and confusing. Be unashamed of the trust you have in Jesus to work all things together for your good. I see so many people who bond with others and start friendships by gossiping or complaining, but usually those friendships don't last. Grumbling will never lead you to God's best. Philippians 2:15 even calls that generation "crooked." Think about how different the world is today from when that was written, but it was still crooked. God is not surprised by how crooked our generation is, but He still calls us to be different. He wants us to "shine among them like stars in the sky" (v. 15). I pray you and I can shine like these stars and make Jesus a little clearer for the others around us.

#5 - The women were joyful about their calling and expectant of joy to come.

We should spend more days rejoicing in who God is than in trying to change who we are in order to be liked. When we see these women, we see two women who talked about what Jesus had done. The woman who touched Jesus' cloak fell to her knees after she was healed as a sign of respect and amazement. The woman at the well went back to the town and told everyone who Jesus was as a sign of rejoicing in who He was and what He did for her.

Rejoicing can be singing and smiling, but it can also be falling to your knees in amazement, praying with thanksgiving midafternoon when a coworker finally opens up, or even calling your grandma to tell her what God is doing in your life. Rejoicing can be dancing, but it can also be whispering to God during the day and writing down a list of the ways God has used you throughout the year. You don't need to be loud to rejoice; you simply have to choose to see God over worldly accomplishments. Rejoice in what God is doing, not what you have done. Rejoicing requires you to pray for eyes that see the world through the lens that God uses. Rejoicing requires you to see that the Lord is near.

Paul also said in Philippians, "Rejoice in the Lord always. I will say it again: Rejoice! Let your gentleness be evident to all. The Lord is near" (4:4–5).

Based on some of the verses Paul wrote, it's hard to believe he wrote the book of Philippians while he was in prison. You may be thinking

How can I rejoice while I'm in a season of loneliness?
How can I rejoice when I hate my school?
How can I rejoice in my season of infertility?

How can I rejoice when my job is demanding?
How can I rejoice when no one seems to like me?
How can I rejoice when my husband left me?
How can I rejoice when I can't find a job?

Paul was choosing to rejoice because of who God was, not because of how the world viewed him. He knew the Lord was near even when his present circumstances were hard. I know you may currently be walking in a season where you not only feel disliked by others but can't help but wonder if God even likes you. You've watched everyone get their answered prayers, while you sit quietly in pain and feel stuck in a hard season.

When the woman at the well was living in sexual sin, God was near, weaving a way for Him to use her for something uniquely purposeful and help her rejoice even in the midst of her bad reputation.

When the woman who touched Jesus' cloak was living isolated from others, God was near, weaving a way for Him to use her boldness and give her a miracle.

When Paul sat in prison after being abused and hurt for his faith, he was writing words we would read more than two thousand years later, and God was near and weaving his story to continue to be one about rejoicing in God's ability to give us boldness even in hard seasons. Even when prison was Paul's location, rejoicing was still his choice.

So when life isn't great, rejoice in who God is and the boldness He can give you. If He can give the woman bleeding for years the courage to leave isolation and seek Jesus, He can give you the boldness you need to see Him. If He can give the woman at the well the courage to go back to her hometown of gossip and judgment and tell them her story and about Jesus, then surely

God can give you boldness to be confident in your purpose. And if Paul could sit in prison, hurt and abused, and rejoice in who God is while trusting that God was making a way when there seemed to be no way, then you and I can also rejoice even in the midst of our hard seasons.

I want boldness for you not because I think it will make you feel better or make your life more wonderful. I want boldness for you because I don't want you to miss out on God doing something big in you and through you for His glory. You have the power to tell others about Christ. You have the opportunity to wake up and feel purpose. You have the chance to rejoice in a hard season. So maybe you and I should care more about being bold than being liked.

And if we are ever in charge of kicking the game-winning point, I pray we are more focused on the goal in front of us than the crowd around us. And maybe that's true for all things. May we focus more on the Savior in front of us than the crowd that may like us or may hate us tomorrow.

PART 6

What Will They Think If My Life Is Transformed?

Mary Magdalene went and announced to the disciples, "I have seen the Lord"—and that he had said these things to her.

JOHN 20:18 (ESV)

CHAPTER 12

Learn from Mary Magdalene

I GREW UP IN SOUTH LOUISIANA. I WENT TO A BIG PUBLIC high school, and I loved it. High school wasn't the best years of my life, but it was transformative and created who I am today. Like many teenagers, in high school, I wanted to be perfect and needed to please others.

This chapter was only going to be about my redemptive story, but then as I was writing it, I received a message from a person I hadn't heard from since high school. I think we sat near each other at lunch sometimes, on the outside patio. I was praying about what story I would share in this chapter but was only thinking of my personal stories. Then Hunter Lyle messaged me.

We grew up in similar families, similar neighborhoods, and the same school. I also was friends with his cousin in high school. I spent my days chasing perfection, chasing the perfect body, and feeling the need to prove everyone wrong. He chased the party lifestyle. It started with marijuana, then he had to repeat junior year because of cocaine, but luckily he got involved with a program at our school that helped students prepare for culinary careers. He graduated with me, and we both tossed our hats in the air at the same time. We left Fontainebleau High with dreams. We both left that stadium wondering what was next for us.

I went on to college, where I started partying too much and blacking out because of alcohol. He went on to work service industry jobs and be a chef at a local high-end restaurant. However, his addiction to cocaine became worse, and my addiction to people pleasing and being someone I wasn't became worse. He transitioned from weed to meth because someone said the high was better. I became obsessed with what others thought about me because I wanted to *be* better. We were now miles away and states away but both struggling to find our place in this world.

Hunter went to jail many times, but he said jail wasn't that bad. He liked the structure, and at that time said he needed someone to tell him what to do. He was in and out of jail, but when at home he was spending his trust fund. Finally, he used up all the money, and once went thirty-two days in his apartment without electricity or plumbing. Thirty-two days. This was in south Louisiana, so it was a big deal. When he said this, I gasped. He was spending all his money on drugs, and when he got his hands on more money, all he could think about was his next high.

When I got money, all I could think about was maybe paying for a certain beauty look, name brand, or skin treatment that could make me hotter, hopefully curing my insecurities. Even today I struggle with thinking, *Yes, I need Botox.* Every time I get a bonus I feel that temptation to buy something extreme to help me look like the world tells me to look. I look at my money and realize I have prioritized changing myself to chase perfection.

Finally, Hunter had a friend at work suggest he use heroin at night to help fall asleep. Since he had tried everything else, he tried heroin and became addicted to that drug. His brother had a son during this time and wouldn't let Hunter meet him. His family created distance but were praying something would change. Hunter was arrested again, but this time he was physically deteriorating and needed help. The judge said he could get out if his dad drove him straight to rehab.

Hunter went to a men's discipleship rehab where he went to church daily. He participated in street evangelism and more. His life changed. He had known of God his whole life, but now he was turning away from shame and sin and a life of chasing a high. He went from chasing a high to chasing a higher purpose. Hunter realized God was real and had a greater purpose for him. He had grown up hearing the gospel but finally truly believed that Jesus conquered the grave for him personally. Hunter knew the gospel and believed in this truth.

I remember struggling with bulimia again after my first book came out. I would eat a lot and feel shame, and even though I knew throwing up wasn't good for me, it was the only thing at that time that made me feel better. I would make myself throw up. This caused harm to my teeth. I went from never having a cavity to having four in one checkup. I finally saw a professional counselor and got help. Around the same time Hunter was finding Christ, I was finally getting the professional help I needed.

On the phone he told me he was two years and almost four months sober. I could sense he was proud of this, but he also talked more about the times he evangelized. He told me once that he was at Walmart with his friend in the program and they asked to pray for a lady. Well, he actually told this lady that his friend, who hadn't publicly prayed for anyone before, wanted to pray for her. He was trying to encourage his friend. She said no. However, after buying her groceries, she came back to the two recovering addicts and said she did want prayer. Her son was an addict and was experiencing brain damage from the drugs. She wanted them to pray for a miracle, so they both did. Two weeks later, this lady came back and said her son was discharged from the hospital and was now healed.

Hunter went from being addicted to drugs to evangelizing in a Walmart. He went from chasing a high to knowing the King who sits on the high throne. Both of us tossed our hats in the air on our graduation day with our dreams and desires. Although our paths were completely different, we both needed redemption. We both needed our good God. Sometimes the boldest thing you can do is accept help. The boldest thing you can do is realize you aren't stuck.

When I think about boldly accepting help, I think of Mary Magdalene. When she met Jesus, she had seven demons possessing her. Some Bible commentators say that the number seven in the Bible refers to something being complete, so having seven demons possessing her would be painful and hard to get out. She must've felt shame and hurt. But Jesus removed those demons, and she was healed. What did she do next? Did she go back home and think, *Thank God I got those demons out*? Did she go on to focus fully on her business and forget about what Jesus did? Was this moment simply a part of her past?

What Mary Magdalene did next is important. She left her home, all she knew, and supported Jesus' ministry financially and with her time. And she was present for some of the most important moments in the gospel. She witnessed Jesus' burial and was there to see His resurrected body at the empty tomb. Jesus wasn't just one moment or interaction for her. It wasn't just one conversation. It wasn't just raising her hand and walking to the altar once. Don't get me wrong, her boldness and healing started with one powerful, redemptive, and healing moment with her Savior. But what happened next is important for us to understand—she followed Jesus.

After this, Jesus traveled from one town and village to another, proclaiming the good news of the kingdom of God. The Twelve were with him, and also some women who had been cured of evil spirits and diseases: Mary (called Magdalene) from whom seven demons had come out; Joanna the wife of Chuza, the manager of Herod's household; Susanna; and many others. These women were helping to support them out of their own means. (Luke 8:1–3)

When we read this passage, we see three things:

Jesus had a lot to do, but He wasn't "too busy."
We were children of God before we were "busy."

So often we use busyness as an excuse. We are basically saying, *I have more important things to do.* Jesus was walking to places, traveling by foot from one village to another, preaching and proclaiming the good news, with people following Him. So often you and I are "too busy" for our boldness. What a shame it would be if we missed out on the adventures of following Jesus because we were too busy.

I get it. We all have a lot of plans, classes, schedules, and systems in our lives, but if we are following a schedule more than we are following Jesus, we have made an idol out of ourselves. The world doesn't need a busy you; the world needs a bold you. This world needs your unique voice and your unique placement to make a difference. Even the smallest things, like who is next to you in line at the grocery store, are for a reason. Never miss out on a conversation because you're too busy.

Jesus saw the one. Jesus saw the hurt Mary Magdalene struggling with seven demons. Jesus sees you right now struggling with anxiety, addiction, insecurity, abuse, depression, and your hurt. He sees you personally and walks up to you individually. Your hurt isn't too small for Jesus, and it definitely is not too big.

You and I must strive to always look for the one hurting each day. Maybe we can bring the blessing that person has been praying for. Pray to have eyes that don't overlook those who are struggling. Pray to discern who needs you to point them to the ultimate Healer, Jesus Christ.

> Women followed Jesus. They were part of this early revival. Women were wanted then by Jesus, and women are wanted now. They were never called to squeeze themselves into these tables; they were offered seats.

There was once a time in my life long ago when I realized I, as a woman, with more or equal education, was getting paid less than a man in my organization. I also realized that no women sat at the tables of the decision-making positions. I was frustrated. It wasn't about the money or wanting to be a big shot; it was more a frustration with knowing that I, as a woman, wasn't wanted. It was easy for me during this time to think God didn't want me on His team as much as a man. But when I see Scripture, I see that women were there, wanted, leaders, and supported. They weren't the same as men because they were each unique and different, but both were valued and needed for Jesus' ministry. Both sexes supported His ministry.

So what does that mean for you and me? We don't have to push ourselves into tables hoping they will give us a chance. Yes, there are still some glass ceilings that need to be shattered, but you can walk with the truth that your Savior walked with women too—women were part of His ministry, and women were welcomed. Work hard, speak up even when that boss's voice feels stronger, but never forget that your Savior, along with His twelve male disciples, also included women like Mary Magdalene, who were part of this revival.

> Mary went from having seven demons cast out of her to walking with Jesus and supporting His ministry. Your boldness starts with an encounter, but it doesn't end there; it is only the beginning.

Hunter told me more stories about evangelism he experienced. Walmart wasn't the only place where he prayed for people. He also told me that after he had changed but still had to appear in court, he helped an older woman know where to go for her granddaughter's misdemeanor charge and reassured her she wouldn't go to jail. This grandmother didn't ask him why he was there, but she asked him if she could pray for him. She prayed for the judge to have grace and see his change. Hunter said it was a reminder that God was at work in his life and was walking with him daily.

When you follow God, you begin to see Him in your everyday life. God likes to give us these moments and encounters I sometimes call "God's smiles," small reminders He is there and cares for us. When Hunter told me all this on the phone, I responded, "It is cool what God did to you two years and four months ago when you chose redemption, met God, and chose sobriety, but it is even cooler to hear how you're walking with God and seeing Him daily now."

I think of myself having to choose redemption again with my eating disorder. Yes, I knew God and accepted His love years ago, but there were areas of my life I hadn't fully given to God. Let me be clear: you and I may always struggle with a mental illness on this side of eternity. Some of us may have healing on this side through a miracle, professional help, and through community, but some of us may have to work daily to stay afloat. There is boldness in realizing our bodies are flawed and true healing will only be delivered in heaven. I get that it's easier to say but harder to live if you're fighting chronic illness, mental illness, or disease, but spiritual redemption is life-changing and something you get to experience. It is beautiful to be free from shame and walk boldly, knowing Jesus paid it all. I know I still have to fight my eating disorder daily, but for whatever you are going through, may we fight our fights, let Jesus take the lead, and trust that spiritual redemption will always be more than enough.

However, we can all be like Mary Magdalene. We can go from chasing the world and being consumed by the Enemy to being a walking warrior for His truth. It is easy to think, *I guess I can be redeemed, but there's no way someone like me could show others how to be redeemed themselves*, but when you listen to those thoughts, you are missing out on true redemption. True redemption comes from Jesus, not you. And when you understand His power, you realize it isn't about being qualified, having the right experience, or being the "perfect church girl" to share His love; it is about knowing the God who can speak through you. God wants you to accept the redemption, then continue walking with Him. He doesn't want you just to accept the redemption; He wants you to witness the mother's prayer at Walmart and her son becoming healed. He wants you to see how He is reaching the recovering addict from your hometown or the innocent girl who seemed to have it all together but fell apart only to find Him. He wants the good girl obsessed with perfection, the one who struggles with alcohol, the drunk guy at the party, the Sunday school teacher secretly battling anxiety, and the mother struggling with knowing her worth. All are wanted not just to feel peace from their Savior but to show others peace.

We will talk in the next chapter about how Mary Magdalene was one of the last at Jesus' burial site and was the first to witness the resurrection. But right now I want to conclude this chapter by reminding you of Jesus' power. Jesus took a woman whom religious leaders scorned for her seven demons, a woman whose past was of struggle, and He transformed her into a bold follower of Him. Maybe you're an introvert and don't think you can be bold, maybe your past is ugly, or maybe you don't think you fit the type of person Jesus would want, but that's Jesus. Jesus wants you and me—women who are a little bit of a mess and a whole lot of struggle. He wants us to accept His redemption and then boldly choose to follow Him.

I pray for boldness in you and through you. I pray you can accept healing and accept the role you are given to join God's team. Life will knock you down, and although Hunter's story and my story were different, we both have the same God and the same redemption Mary Magdalene had over two thousand years ago. The Lord wants to heal you so you can walk into God's purpose for you too.

CHAPTER 13

Five Reasons
I Choose to
"Go and Tell"

THE BIBLE DOESN'T TELL US MUCH ABOUT MARY Magdalene during Jesus' life on earth besides that she was healed by Jesus, supported His ministry financially, and walked with Him. She was redeemed and then joined His team. But when the crucifixion happened, we read that she was present. John 19:25 says, "Near the cross of Jesus stood his mother, his mother's sister, Mary the wife of Clopas, and Mary Magdalene."

I can't help but think about what it was like for Mary Magdalene to be next to those who loved Jesus so much, knew Him so well, and were changed by Him to see Him die a painful death. His execution wasn't an injection or a quick gunshot. The women stood there and watched Jesus die the slow and painful death of crucifixion. They knew He was good, but they also knew not everyone liked Him. The crowd had just chosen to save Barabbas, a convicted violent criminal, over Jesus, a guy who rubbed the religious leaders the wrong way. Mary Magdalene was there, and she witnessed Jesus die a painful death.

In Mark 15, we see that Mary Magdalene and Mary the mother of Jesus were some of the last people to see Jesus' body.

And when evening had come, since it was the day of Preparation, that is, the day before the Sabbath, Joseph of Arimathea, a respected member of the council, who was also himself looking for the kingdom of God, took courage and went to Pilate and asked for the body of Jesus. Pilate was surprised to hear that he should have already died. And summoning the centurion, he asked him whether he was already dead. And when he learned from the centurion that he was dead, he granted the corpse to Joseph. And Joseph bought a linen shroud, and taking him down, wrapped him in the linen shroud and laid him in a tomb that had been cut out of the rock. And he rolled a stone against the entrance of the tomb. Mary Magdalene and Mary the mother of Joses saw where he was laid. (vv. 42–47 ESV)

Jesus wasn't just dead; His body was prepared for burial and placed in the tomb. His body was cleaned, but His scars were still present. It must have been heartbreaking watching Him take His final breath, anguishing in pain, but it was probably more chilling for Mary Magdalene to help prepare His body and watch a stone finally separate her from the man who saved her.

For that silent Saturday Mary must've thought about that stone separating her Savior from her. But the story wasn't over. Mary Magdalene's purpose had just begun, and she was going to learn about the boldness inside her. First Mary Magdalene noticed the empty tomb.

Early on the first day of the week, while it was still dark, Mary Magdalene went to the tomb and saw that the stone had been removed from the entrance. So she came running to Simon Peter and the other disciple, the one Jesus loved, and said, "They have taken the Lord out of the tomb, and we don't know where they have put him!" (John 20:1–2)

There Mary Magdalene was, back to care for Jesus' tomb, and she noticed the stone was rolled away. This stone in front of the tomb was so heavy that it was almost impossible to roll it away. She assumed that, as a final act of disrespect, others who hated Jesus took away His body. She told Peter and John, two of Jesus' disciples, about the stone being rolled away, and they ran to see the tomb was empty.

> Now Mary stood outside the tomb crying. As she wept, she bent over to look into the tomb and saw two angels in white, seated where Jesus' body had been, one at the head and the other at the foot. They asked her, "Woman, why are you crying?" "They have taken my Lord away," she said, "and I don't know where they have put him." At this, she turned around and saw Jesus standing there, but she did not realize that it was Jesus. He asked her, "Woman, why are you crying? Who is it you are looking for?" Thinking he was the gardener, she said, "Sir, if you have carried him away, tell me where you have put him, and I will get him." Jesus said to her, "Mary." She turned toward him and cried out in Aramaic, "Rabboni!" (which means "Teacher"). Jesus said, "Do not hold on to me, for I have not yet ascended to the Father. Go instead to my brothers and tell them, 'I am ascending to my Father and your Father, to my God and your God.'" Mary Magdalene went to the disciples with the news: "I have seen the Lord!" And she told them that he had said these things to her. (John 20:11–18)

Mary was distraught, and even though she saw two angels, she wept and assumed someone had taken her Savior's body from the tomb. She then met a man she thought was the gardener, and she asked Him where He had taken Jesus' body. But all it took was

Jesus saying "Mary" for her to respond "Teacher!" She knew He was her Teacher and Savior.

Jesus told her to go and tell the disciples the news that He had risen and was ascending to God. He then said, "I am ascending to my Father and your Father, to my God and your God" (v. 17). I love that Jesus reminded her that He, the blameless Savior who healed her, shared the same God with her. He called God "my God and your God." I like to think Jesus is looking at you and me right now and reminding us He is with *our* God.

Mary Magdalene went and told Peter and John the news. Was she worried about whether they would listen to a woman? She was in a culture where women weren't educated. Women were not taken seriously. But she was too focused on being bold and doing what the Lord called her to do to care about what they would think.

The world may not take you seriously, but I pray you see that your Savior seriously loves you. He wants you, and He calls you up. Your gender does not hinder you from being used for the gospel. We serve a Savior who had women on His team and gave them important roles. Jesus never boxed women in; He called them up. Jesus is also calling you up right now to live boldly for Him.

I want you to live a life that "goes and tells." Even though I am an extrovert, "going and telling" isn't always easy for me. It requires prayer, confidence, and a little bit of crazy. I have to be prepared for these moments. I am not always good at this, but there was one time that had an impact on me when I was getting my nails done. I was in a job where I made very little money and I lived with a sweet couple because I couldn't afford rent in the area yet. While getting my nails done, which was a treat for me, a lady was talking about a stroke she had just had. She looked to be about my mother's age and I felt God calling me to pay for her pedicure. I didn't want to do it. I wanted Chick-fil-A after and knew if I did this, I wouldn't have money for lunch. But it wouldn't leave my mind. I knew I needed to pay for her pedicure. I finally caved and prayed to God, "I'll do it but then I'm heading out; that is it." I finally did it and told her before I left that I was paying for her. She started crying and then she asked, "Why did you do this for me?"

Dang it, God . . . I just wanted to listen, buy the pedicure, and leave. I knew what I had to say next.

I had to tell her why. And even though I did say she reminded me of my mother, I also told her I wouldn't have done this if it wasn't for what Jesus did on the cross and a conversation I felt I had with God. I told her I felt God nudge me to do this. I told her how God sent His Son who paid the price for my sins, and I believe in the gospel and what Jesus did, so I strive to live out His love. I told her how the gospel changed my life in a short amount of time. She nodded and said, "Thanks for sharing that with me."

I was even more upset after that because all I got was a "thanks for sharing that with me." But that day God reminded me I am called to "go and tell" not for results but for opportunities. We've all heard the "I may just be planting a seed," but sometimes I am truly just tilling the soil. I may not get a "yes, now I believe!" But I get to make God's name grow in a small way that might lead to big life change.

You, too, are called to "go and tell," and it can feel weird. But here are five reason we "go and tell":

#1 - Wisdom comes from prayer and God.

When we look at the world through wisdom, we see that the wise choice we make isn't where we go to college or where we work. The wisest choice we make is how we communicate with Jesus.

Something embarrassing about me is that before my first kiss I googled "how to kiss a boy." Yes, this is cringy, and I am praying my family doesn't read this part, but I know they will. We live in a world that says you can google for wisdom, but this isn't true. We look to the internet for advice, seek wisdom from our inner selves, and wait for permission before doing anything.

In a world where people think you can get wisdom online about your future decisions, remember true wisdom and discernment about what you should do comes from the Holy Spirit. The Holy Spirit makes you bold, not cowardly. You may still be fearful, but you can run to your calling. Mary Magdalene went and told others about Jesus' resurrection and was the first evangelist.

#2 - "Going and telling" is not normal, but normal is boring. If you try to be normal, you'll miss out on opportunities.

I love to write, and before I wrote books, I wrote a blog. There were two fraternity guys in college who would make fun of it. I almost let their opinion of my blog stop me from writing, which was something God was calling me to do. I remember crying to my college roommates about their mean comments. However, one of them looked at me and said, "If God's calling you to write, allow that voice to be louder than anyone who says you shouldn't.

And get ready, this guy won't be the last to doubt you or make fun of you."

She was right—he wasn't the last person to make fun of my writing. There were plenty of others, but I began to look at their opinions differently because God's voice became louder. And when God's voice became louder, I became bolder.

I knew a guy at college who liked to make music. He wanted to make music that made people happy. There was a Twitter account about Baylor students, and someone called his music horrible. In 2020, the band he started after college produced a song that went viral on TikTok with him as the lead singer. The other songs on the album were a hit too. Their album did amazing, and they were invited to sing at many well-known music festivals. Every time I see his song in an Instagram story, I smile. I wonder what the people who tweeted about him are doing now. Imagine what would've happened if he had let that tweet be louder than the call he felt from God. The world would've missed out on his gift, and he would've missed out on blessings from the Lord that came from being bold.

#3 - Scripture says it is our calling as disciples.

Matthew 28:19–20 says, "Therefore go and make disciples of all nations, baptizing them in the name of the Father and of the Son and of the Holy Spirit, and teaching them to obey everything I have commanded you. And surely I am with you always, to the very end of the age."

Jesus said this to the disciples after He rose from the dead. Mary had already told the disciples what Jesus had done, and He had repaired and shared moments with all the disciples. Jesus quite literally came back to show them the good news and to remind them they were called to share that good news. But when He said this, He wasn't referring only to those disciples. He was referring to all of us. The chain of discipleship is beautiful. It starts with an older woman pouring into a young mom, who pours into both her child and a girl she leads in a Bible study, who then grows up and pours into other young girls. Discipleship makes a lasting impact. And Jesus promised He would be there for all this.

Making disciples starts with boldness. Maybe you will do this at your job, through your art, or through teaching a Bible study. However you do it, you're called to do it in the name of the Lord. And when you do it, make sure you're listening to Jesus and not the opinions of others. Being bold is worth it. Being bold leads to unexpected adventures and heaven becoming a little more crowded.

#4 – "Going and telling" leads us to adventures.

When you "go and tell," you may end up in a crazy, unexpected place. I have one friend named Sophie, and she always thought she would get married and live near family in Florida. God called the man who became her husband to be a missionary in Thailand. She obviously prayed through it and trusted God was leading them there. Then while there she agreed to be a foster mom based on a feeling she had that maybe God was calling her to this. She had wanted to have kids young in marriage but thought this would be a good opportunity to make a difference. She ended up getting the call to foster twins in Thailand. She didn't know why God had called her husband and her to Thailand at first, and there are many reasons why, but when she rocks those children and sings "Jesus Loves Me" to them, I know she knows that "going and telling" all nations leads to unexpected adventures.

Sometimes the adventure isn't always fostering twins in Thailand; sometimes the adventure is simply a late-night drive that sparks a conversation about Jesus, running a half-marathon with a friend and using it as a bridge to talk about our Creator, or even just driving the girl who drank too much home. Adventure isn't just in the big trips; it is in any trip that ends with an unexpected conversation about Jesus.

#5 - "Going and telling" leads us to true empowerment.

Women empowerment is great, but I think we forget who truly holds the power. Do you want to know what is more empowering than a crazy song, a dance trend, a good workout, or a promotion? Knowing that I can point others to the more powerful One and do life with the highest power. People will try to tell you women empowerment comes from a feeling or from hitting a goal, but when I think about Mary running to tell the men what she saw, I see true women empowerment. I see men listening to her and I see a bold woman who is empowered by her Savior. Seriously, picture her running to them, not worried about how she looks or what others think. She was solely focused on the good news. I hope my heart can be empowered by the good news in this way. I know my heart can be empowered when I also "go and tell."

Your most important calling is to go and tell. Your voice isn't meant to be silenced. When God calls you to something, I pray you do it. However, don't expect a literal voice; sometimes it is just your heart pumping with joy as you paint, teach, start that business, care for your children, make music, or write. When you feel this joy, do it for Jesus. Find ways to go and tell with this gift. But never forget we all have the gift of our voice. We all are called to spread the gospel through love and through this truth.

And in a world where you feel like women aren't treated fairly, I want you to remember that in a time when women weren't respected, the disciples knew the good news was first shared by a woman. The women were the last with Jesus' body and the first to see Jesus' resurrection. Women aren't an afterthought in Scripture. In fact, Jesus intentionally chose them to be warriors of truth.

Maybe you're someone who feels silenced. Don't listen to the fake "wisdom" that comes from this world that tells you that your gift, your opinion, and your voice need to be silenced. In a world that tells you to go home, your Savior says, *Go and tell.* When people make you feel weird for using your gifts, drown out their opinions with your Teacher's voice. He called Mary Magdalene by name, and she was able to recognize Him. I pray you and I may know the Lord's voice and tug on our hearts so well that when He simply says our names, we recognize Him. And on the days we don't know what we are called to do, I pray we do what Mary and many others did: tell others about Jesus, love big, and make disciples. We know about Jesus' teaching today because Mary was bold. Her boldness changed thousands of generations. Your boldness can do the same.

While you're being bold, don't forget that Jesus isn't just

sitting in heaven thinking, *Good luck out there being bold in your corporate job!* No, He said, "I am with you always, to the very end of the age." Even though the task feels hard, our Savior is great. He isn't just in heaven wishing us good luck; He's walking with us always.

PART 7

What Will They Think If I'm Ordinary?

In Joppa there was a disciple named Tabitha; . . . she was always doing good and helping the poor.

ACTS 9:36

CHAPTER 14

Learn from Tabitha

MY FRIENDS WHO KNOW ME BEST HAVE HEARD ME SAY, "If I have a daughter one day, I could see myself naming her Tabitha!"

I know what you're thinking: Yes, that's a pretty name, but for a grandma. I bet she'd be friends with Betty and play bingo at her retirement community. It's a cute name, but it doesn't scream a girl in kindergarten in 2030 wearing pigtails.

Let me explain. In 2020 I was frustrated and overwhelmed. I was busy, and then this thing called COVID happened, and suddenly life flipped. I felt purposeful in my job and then was furloughed. I didn't live with anyone for the first two months of COVID, and as a single young woman, that season was hard. I felt alone and overwhelmed at what my purpose was. I felt small and easily forgotten. I kept wondering, *How the heck am I supposed to do big things when I live alone and can't even leave my house?*

Then I met Tabitha in the pages of Acts.

In the city of Joppa there was a follower named Tabitha (whose Greek name was Dorcas). She was always doing good deeds and kind acts. While Peter was in Lydda, Tabitha became sick and died. Her body was washed and put in a room upstairs. Since Lydda is near Joppa and the followers in Joppa heard that Peter was in Lydda, they sent two messengers to Peter. They begged him, "Hurry, please come to us!" So Peter got ready and went with them. When he arrived, they took him to the upstairs room where all the widows stood around Peter, crying. They showed him the shirts and coats Tabitha had made when she was still alive. Peter sent everyone out of the room and kneeled and prayed. Then he turned to the body and said, "Tabitha, stand up." She opened her eyes, and when she saw Peter, she sat up. He gave her his hand and helped her up. Then he called the saints and the widows into the room and showed them that Tabitha was alive. (9:36–41 NCV)

Some of you may be wondering why I chose to write about Tabitha. There are women who have a lot more written about them. I mean, there are only six verses about her. We don't hear anything about her again. There are women we know more about historically and biblically. Yet during 2020 Tabitha changed my outlook on life.

Tabitha was a woman who lived near the coast and had a gift for sewing. Back in that day, widows were overlooked. There was no life insurance or government program that was available to help them. The book of Acts takes place after Jesus rose from the dead and appeared to the disciples. It's a book all about the church and the gospel growing as the disciples were basically like, *Yeah, that happened, Jesus rose from the dead, so let's do what He prepared for us to do and tell the world.* The book of Acts is also set in an interesting time when politically and religiously things were changing. The Christian movement was spreading quickly in the book of Acts, but oftentimes the government was run by old "religious" Jewish Pharisees. Widows were sometimes helped by the Jewish government leaders, but if they became Christian, they couldn't receive the little help they were given.

Peter followed what Jesus had commissioned them to do and was traveling through a town when people approached him, crying about how Tabitha, a beloved member of the church, had died.

I want you to picture the scene. Tabitha was pronounced dead, and her body was in a room upstairs being cleaned. The widows and poor were wearing clothes Tabitha had made them. When they heard Peter was in a city nearby called Lydda, they sent two messengers to tell him Tabitha had died and convince him to hurry to Joppa. These cities were close, but they were still over fourteen miles apart. That means the messengers had to walk twenty-eight miles. It took me over two hours to run a half-marathon once. Peter, though, knew he was supposed to go see Tabitha and the other widows, and he walked the fourteen miles to see Tabitha's body. What do you think they talked about as they walked miles to Joppa? I don't know, but they did know that Peter, someone who had walked with Jesus and was spreading the gospel, needed to see Tabitha.

When Peter got upstairs, the widows and the poor showed Peter the shirts and coats Tabitha had made them. I don't think this was like a TikToker's fashion haul. They weren't saying, "I got the best deal from this designer named Tabitha. It is one of a kind!" They were crying as they showed him the coats that helped them get through winters, the shirts that made them feel human when others overlooked them, and the tangible evidence that Tabitha loved them. Their clothes showed that Tabitha wanted them to feel valued, seen, and cared for. Her clothes took time to make. She could have sold them, traded them, or taken advantage of the poor who were in desperate need of her service, but she didn't. These garments were more than just clothes; they were signs of Tabitha's love and service to her Savior.

Peter talked to those crying over her death and sent them out. He then raised Tabitha from the dead by the power of Jesus Christ, then helped her up.

I want us to think about several things we can learn from Tabitha:

Tabitha didn't have many lines.

We never hear Tabitha's response. We don't know what she looked like, how much money she had, or if she was married. She didn't get a book of the Bible named after her, and she wasn't the author of her account. But what matters is that we know of her faith and that she loved others well. She used her gift to serve her neighbors. She wasn't trying to be the main character. And her looks, money, and romantic relationship didn't matter. What mattered was that she knew that Jesus was the main character, and she loved others as He did.

Tabitha loved the overlooked and loved her city well.

In a world where we dream of going viral and reaching millions of people in an instant, it's easy for us to forget the most important calling we all have. If you can't love your neighbor well, how can you love a stranger? If a neighbor is a stranger to you, how can you say you're trying to love the world and make the world a better place? There's something so beautiful about the widowed, the poor, and the overlooked feeling seen by Tabitha, and when she died, they cherished the fabrics she had spent hours sewing for them. I hope when I leave this earth, and my time is done, my neighbors remember me as the girl who tried to love them like Jesus would.

Peter helped Tabitha up after Jesus raised her from the dead.

After Peter prayed and the Holy Spirit brought Tabitha to life, there's a powerful moment when Peter reached to help Tabitha come out of the bed she had been dead in. Tabitha, someone who loved others well, still needed someone's help. We so often want to be independent, but when we are going through hardships, we forget that we need someone to pray for us, go to Jesus with us through prayer, and even physically help us when it is time to get up. I've had friends help me up after breakups, hardships, job loss, moments of worry, and loneliness. We need Christian friends, the church, mentors, and even fellow believers we don't know well to help us. I love being a strong, independent woman. You can listen to girl-power music, work out, stay healthy, make your own money, and figure out how to girl-boss, but there will still be a day when you need someone to help you up. On that day make sure you are humble enough to grab the hand of a fellow believer.

Tabitha, an ordinary woman who loved big and knew her big God, was raised from the dead because of Jesus' power.

Like Tabitha, you, too, have the power to go from death to new life. I don't mean literally, even though Christ can do anything; I mean spiritually. When we accept Christ as our Savior, we are like Tabitha and rise from being spiritually dead. The old life of sin and shame we had is gone, and the new life of freedom and grace begins. I think we forget how powerful our Savior is. He reigns in heaven yet gives us new mercies each day (Lam. 3:22–23). If you want to walk boldly, make sure you're walking new. Make sure your soul has become new and you've acknowledged how powerful your Savior is. Before you can change the world, you have to walk with the One who saved the world.

If you don't love the overlooked, you're missing out.

We are in a culture where people try to be the best and look out for themselves only. However, looking out for the overlooked gives you true purpose and meaning. Your life was never meant to be about being liked; it was about being love. Being love for the person you bump into at the grocery store, the teen who hits the bumper on your car, the guy who lost his job, the homeless family on the street, or the fourteen-year-old feeling insecure and needing a mentor. Look out for the overlooked, show them they are seen, and focus more on living love than being liked.

Maybe you're reading this book because you want your life to have meaning. But if you want your life to have true purpose and meaning, you have to stop living for yourself. You have to stop trying to be big and love others big instead. You may never be as known as your favorite pop star, sell as many books as Oprah, or meet a president. But you can leave this world and know you loved the overlooked, and you loved those around you.

There was a girl in high school who could never remember my name freshman year. This popular brunette was on the cheerleading team and got paired with me for a science project. I'll never forget how my heart dropped when I heard her go over to some other cool girl and ask, "Which one is Grace Valentine? I hate when I get paired with random people."

Fast-forward to about four years later when I went shopping at a boutique in my hometown. I walked in and this girl, now a cute and trendy woman, looked at me and said, "Wait, I know you. You went to Fontainebleau High, right? Didn't we do a project together?"

I reminded her of my name, then she turned to her mother, also shopping with her, and said, "Grace was always so kind to everyone. I'll never forget her looking out for some of the students with learning disabilities in our class freshman year."

Wait, Miss Cheerleader who called me "random" remembers who I talked to in class? She may not have remembered my name, but she remembered my actions. She may not remember how hard I worked on that science project, but she remembered that I was kind. Maybe it didn't matter if she remembered me. She may not have known my name, but she knew my love.

I'm sure there is also someone who could tell you they'll never forget about a time I was the opposite of kind as well. But here's what that cheerleader reminded me of that day in the boutique: it is better for your love to be known than for you to be known. The truth we all hate to admit is that one day we will die. How sad would it be if two thousand people came to your funeral but no one had a story about a time when you were kind? No one is going to be talking about how hot you were at twenty-one at your funeral. No one will care about how many promotions you got. But they will care about how you treated them. Leave that kind of legacy.

In a world where everyone wants to be known and be a main character, I hope we live to make Jesus' name known. I hope we find purpose in the gifts God has given us and steward them to those who need them most. Tabitha made clothes for the poor because sewing was a gift the Lord had given her. If you can write, write a letter to someone struggling. If you can change a tire, when you see someone struggling on the side of the road, help them. Whatever you do, whatever gift you have, serve others and love the vulnerable with this gift.

And on the mornings when you wonder if your life matters, I pray you look up. Your God is looking down on you, giving you each breath, reminding you that He's not finished with you. Tabitha was still living because God wasn't finished with her yet. Maybe she had more clothes to sew, or maybe she was going to start sharing her testimony of new life with others. Some mornings may suck, but even they are meaningful because God has purposefully put you where you are. Trust Him.

CHAPTER 15

Five Things Better than Being Known

THERE'S THIS WEIRD KIND OF PRESSURE I FEEL TO BE THE first person on the dance floor at a wedding. I don't know why I feel this way. I feel like the whole vibe of a dance floor is dependent on me sometimes. As if I'm the "director of fun" organizing the dance to "Cotton-Eye Joe" at a wedding. But the truth is, the wedding would be just fine without me. No one needs me there— I'm not the bride, for goodness' sake. I'm just a girl at table eight.

I don't know why I feel the need to be the leader in these situations. The truth is, no one cares if I'm dancing. They'll dance if they want. I just feel like I want to be the one; I want to be the one who makes things happen, lights up the room, and makes the atmosphere better. I want to do all the things needed to make all the people think, *Thank God Grace Valentine is here!*

At work, I feel this way too. I sometimes get stressed about my many jobs and my inability to be everything to everyone. As I write this book, I am juggling a lot. I have to maintain three jobs to pay my mortgage so I can chase my dream of writing full-time. There's this rumor that after you write one book, you're rich. I can promise you that is false. My old Honda Civic is tangible proof. Some boys from my hometown hit me up two years ago after they googled my net worth and some random website said I was worth millions. This is fake news. If I was worth millions, would I still have babysitting jobs on Friday nights as a twenty-five-year-old? Probably not. But if the former baseball boys from my hometown ask, maybe let's keep them thinking I'm rich; it is kind of funny.

Like many of you, I'm busy. I want to please all the people I work for. I want to be an amazing worker. I want to be known by them as important.

Because of this desire to please others, I recently had a breakdown from exhaustion. I felt like so many people depended on me. I seemed to never be able to catch up on my emails, texts, or the demands from others. I felt so much pressure to make everyone else's job easier, be the best worker, and still manage a social life. I had a friend tell me point-blank, "Grace, everyone will be fine without you, and you don't have to be known for doing it all. Aren't you forgetting what really matters?"

I hate to admit it, but even though I was burnt out from being needy and doing a lot, I wanted to be needed and wanted. I wanted to be well-liked and known for doing all the things. But during this season, I forgot the most important calling.

I hope you are known by those you trust. I hope your friends know your Chipotle order and get on to you for texting that guy you shouldn't be talking to. I pray you find people you can be honest with and people who can read the frustration on your face after a hard day. I pray you are known by them. But I pray you and I can also realize we are not on this earth to be all the things for all the people. We can't be known and truly serve the opinions of others. That's not our job.

When we look at Tabitha, we see a woman who didn't have a whole book of the Bible dedicated to her story; she had only a couple of verses. She didn't rise to high leadership, and we don't know if she was popular with the "cool" peers. Scripture never talks about whether she was married, stylish, or if she was the first on the dance floor at a wedding. We don't know the details about Tabitha, but we do know that she was kind and served the overlooked. She cared for the people others had forgotten.

She wasn't worried about making herself popular; she focused on knowing her neighbors and loving them like Jesus.

We don't know if Tabitha would've been the girl who joined all the clubs, served for the PTA, or made the best bread in town. But we know she loved big. She didn't care if she was known; she was too preoccupied caring for others.

So in honor of Tabitha, let's talk about five things I would rather be than known.

#1 - I would rather be raised to a new life than be known.

Peter, through Jesus' power, raised Tabitha from the dead. She was already pronounced dead, and by the time Peter walked the many miles to get to her, she had been dead for a while. But God wasn't finished with her yet, and the Holy Spirit raised her from the dead. I would rather have the powerful Spirit in me than try to be powerful in my community. When you know Jesus and have faith, you'll do crazier and cooler things than you would if you lived a life trying to be popular.

We can all be raised from the dead spiritually as our souls are raised to new life. In this life we should care about loving big, not being big. In this life we should care about pointing to the most powerful One, not trying to find power and popularity. You may never be the CEO or run the world, but you can be the one who is raised to new life. That one is cooler.

Colossians 3:1 says, "Since you have been raised to new life with Christ, set your sights on the realities of heaven, where Christ sits in the place of honor at God's right hand" (NLT). Allow

Jesus to raise you to new life. This new life will be more about being love than proving to others that you are worth loving. This new life sets your mind on Christ. This new life is one of boldness and the realization that you are no longer trapped in a need for approval. This new life is one that exists to glorify Jesus.

#2 - I would rather be the kindest person in the room than the most popular.

Whenever I speak to high schoolers, I remind them that their homecoming dance is not the Met Gala. You're not going to the Grammys; you're going to a high school dance in the cafeteria. There is no need to be exclusive. No matter what state I am in, there are always going to be high schoolers who tell others, "There's not enough room in our group!" There is always more room; these people are just choosing to leave others out.

At one event, I said this and I saw a group of high school girls laugh and look at one another. They were all so pretty and cute and reminded me of the girls who bullied me growing up. I just knew these girls were the ones who left others out. But they lined up to talk to me after I was done speaking, and I asked them if they were the girls who left someone out. I was going to apologize for being harsh, but to my surprise, *they* were the ones who were left out. Some girl made a list of people invited to her house before homecoming, and all five of these adorable girls were told they didn't make the cut. So instead, they created their own group where everyone was welcome. They didn't have many people, but they had fun.

They said, "But we didn't have dates." I looked at these

beautiful girls and said, "But you had kindness, and that matters more."

So, to you, your kindness will always matter more.

Tabitha had someone who walked twenty-eight miles just to potentially heal her. She must've really made a difference. And I doubt it was because of her fashion impact from sewing: "Tabitha can't leave yet; I need her to sew me this season's new jacket!" All joking aside, she obviously made an impact. Tabitha showed faith and the love of Jesus so well that others believed the disciples could heal her when she was already washed and pronounced dead.

I struggle with leaving a room and wanting to know if I was known and liked. *Did they think I was cool? Did they like me? Did they think my hair was ugly?* Sounds silly because it is silly, but it is true. Something I've been trying to work on is focusing more on leaving love rather than worrying about leaving with a great reputation, good looks, a successful image, or being known by everyone. Leave each room kinder, and always be the one who invites and cares. Don't leave trying to be known.

#3 - I would rather know the overlooked than strive to make my name known.

Tabitha didn't just love her neighbor; she loved the neighbors others overlooked. The widows and poor went unnoticed back in this culture, but she made them feel known.

I was once asked how to reach those who are interested in Christ. My response was simple: just be interested in them. If you believe in Jesus, then you know that Jesus is interested in you, me, the girl who is crying about that guy, the guy who wonders what his purpose is, the friend who is in a hard season, and anyone and everyone. We know Christ is interested in them, even if they have no desire to know Christ. Therefore, the easiest way to reach others and show them the love of Jesus is to be interested in their lives. What hobbies do they enjoy and what trust issues do they have? Have friendships come easily for them or are they difficult? What about their jobs makes them feel purposeful and what is draining them? What are their goals in life? Are they honestly happy on a Wednesday morning?

Jesus sat with people and shared meals with them. Jesus knew the hearts of others. And Tabitha chose to live a life that looked at the overlooked and said, *Hey, I see you.* Her loving others in this way caused them to know Christ and attest to Peter that she made a difference through her big love.

How can you be more interested in the overlooked?

The overlooked had nothing to give in return to Tabitha. They couldn't offer her popularity or a promotion. But she loved them because Tabitha knew the Author of love. Our Savior died for us when we had nothing to give. We were broken sinners and He was perfect, but we needed perfect blood to be shed for our sins. He gave Himself and created love that day He stretched out His arms, saying, *I love you this much,* only to have them nailed to a tree.

As 1 John 4:19 says, "We love because he first loved us." We should walk in love because Jesus hung on a tree in the name of love. True love doesn't love because it gets anything in return. You have people around you in your neighborhood like Tabitha did. You have people who feel forgotten and overlooked. There is someone you may meet today at the grocery store or at the park who feels lonely and forgotten. You can be the blessing they have been praying for.

#4 - I would rather give my gifts to God than make my gifts about me.

When I was fifteen, I had a cool college counselor at summer camp named Keri. I was bad at doing my hair, and though I love my mom and she has so many other talents, so was she. But there was one time at camp when Keri brushed and braided my hair. There were lots of knots. There was probably dirt and weird camp juice mixed in my hair. But she sat there, right before we went to bed, and brushed and braided my hair. Though I was fifteen years old, I still craved this comfort. The comfort of knowing that Keri cared for me, used her time to hang out with me, and tangibly loved me through brushing out those knots affected me forever.

I think we sometimes forget the gifts we serve with don't have to be some crazy talent, even though it can be. I knew an orthodontist who gave someone who grew up in a lower-income home free braces. I knew a doctor who left his medical practice to open one for those without insurance. I knew someone who made flower bouquets and donated them to a nonprofit for helping families adopt. Your gift and talent can be your job or position, but it can also be spending time talking to a struggling teenager. It can be helping the church clean up after an event. It can be a grand gesture that is unique to you or simply an eager heart that helps at the right place and right time.

Tabitha knew how to sew clothes, so she sewed clothes for

others. It was as simple as that. There is a gift you have. Maybe you're amazing at organizing or you know how to cut hair. Maybe you're good at styling outfits or interior decorating. Maybe you're gifted at listening or writing encouraging letters. Whatever it is, remember your gifts should never be about what they can do to make you known, but they should be about what you can do to make your God known. Live for the Giver.

First Peter 4:10 says, "Each of you should use whatever gift you have received to serve others, as faithful stewards of God's grace in its various forms." You should honor God by using the gift He gave you to serve the Giver of life. This doesn't mean if you paint you can only paint pictures of crosses. But make sure your gift brings life and light into this dark world. It doesn't have to scream Jesus, but make sure it shares a message of the hope of the gospel and not one of despair. This world needs more light. Bring this light through unexpected blessings.

#5 - I would rather know my big God than try to be big. I would rather do holy things than main-character things.

I am either the most insecure person in this world or way too confident. It is easy for me to overthink my role for a wedding dance, so you can bet it is easy for me to overthink the role God has given me. We live in a culture that tells girls they need to be the "main character," and frankly, I think this is destructive logic. When you view yourself as the main character of your story, you view your God as less. He is the hero. We were never called to be the main character or the hero. We were called to do holy things, not main-character things.

Tabitha loved big because she was more focused on being holy than being the hero. She knew only Jesus could save these people, but she wanted to love them like Jesus with nothing given back in return. She wasn't trying to be popular; she was just trying to be love. Tabitha probably would be shocked to think you're reading a chapter about her in a book. She was humble to the calling she was given. She didn't ask Jesus to give her a role where she could travel more or be in the spotlight. I pray we focus more on shining Jesus' light than being in the spotlight.

James 4:10 says, "Humble yourselves before the Lord, and he will lift you up." I love that this verse tells us that when we are humble before the Lord, realizing He is bigger and more worthy of worship than us, our Lord will lift us up. This lifting up is more freeing than dancing on the elevated surface at the frat party and goes higher than the pop star does on her floating stage. This "lift" gives us an eternal mindset even in a broken and temporary world.

This world is temporary, and our calling is important. May we be humble enough to know Jesus is the hero. May we shine His light more than we search for our spotlight.

You are meant for more in your life. You are meant to live life boldly. But the boldest thing you can do is realize that this life is about something more important than you. I pray you close this chapter and look for a way to love the overlooked. I pray you do holy things, not main-character things. But mainly I pray you see that you can be like Tabitha today. Whatever gift you have, steward this gift and love others through it. When you wonder why you're here, look at your feet. See where you are? Each day is a gift, and your Savior is giving you an opportunity to bring hope to a hopeless world. You can do big things if you know your big God, but never forget: big things are holy things, not main-character things.

Forty Reminders When You Care About What Others Think

ALL RIGHT, MY LITTLE PEOPLE PLEASERS–OR SHOULD I say, recovering people pleasers and now bold warriors. You did it. You almost finished this book! Maybe you started reading feeling stuck in your current situation or strangled by fear. Maybe you felt trapped in your frustrations or shame. Maybe you felt under-qualified, overcaffeinated, and overwhelmed. Whether you're a high school student struggling with insecurity, a college student triggered by Canvas notifications, a young mother who prays for a successful nap, or a businesswoman trying to prove yourself daily, I pray you will realize your purpose is to live a loving life and not to prove you're worth loving. I pray you remember you were loved by your God before you were needed by your crazy schedule. You were cared for by your Creator before you were busy. I pray you will let God write your story and trust Him when it is a hard chapter. I pray you'll choose boldness and realize it is only a hard chapter and not a bad story.

The women in the Bible were all broken like you and me. They weren't perfect, and some of them had to learn their lessons the hard way. Some were ninety years old and others were fourteen. Some were rich and some felt forgotten. Some had one small gift like sewing and some were political leaders in their community. But they all needed their God and can teach us how to live a bold life.

Then there's you. As you read this last part of the book, I hope you realize God is using you. He is telling a story that others read daily through interactions with you. I do not want you to miss out on what God is doing because you're too scared. I do not want you to miss out on God's best because you're trying to make others like you the best. So read and believe these forty reminders:

1. Life isn't about living for someday; life is what you're doing today. Pray for boldness today. Your life isn't meant to be a ladder climbing up to a career, a relationship, or a social standing; your life is a gift and an opportunity to point others to the Giver.

2. Some days you may need to cry. But always allow your boldness, not your tears, to be your song and anthem. Your tears are a part of your struggle, but your God is a part of your song. Trust that your life will sing praises more than it cries.

3. It isn't a sin to be sad. Some days you may need to be at the feet of Jesus. Oftentimes Jesus gives us moments with Him at His feet to prepare us for something big. Your tears are leading you to your purpose and to your song of deliverance.

4. There will always be some girl out there who just doesn't like you and some silly boy who misses out on you. Stop wasting energy and time trying to convince these people to like you. You are not a restaurant waiting on a review or a product to be enjoyed; you are a daughter of Christ. Remind yourself on the days you feel unliked that your Savior died for you.

5. It's normal to forget things each day. Like those clothes you left in the washer that need to be switched to the dryer—or rewashed. Or that text you thought you replied to but didn't. You forget a lot of things, but don't forget

your time with Jesus. I would hate if you were too busy for your Savior tomorrow. Find time to honestly pray and read Scripture each day. Make it a habit.

6. Redemption is more powerful than your reputation. Remember this and truly believe it.

7. No one really thinks about you as much as you do. And your God thinks about you every second of every moment. He thinks about you and chooses you each moment. Be thankful for this. And when you overthink a conversation, a friendship, or a rejection, remind yourself that the other person probably already forgot about it.

8. Do holy things more than you strive to do likeable things. Holy things aren't "big-deal things." Yes, it could be starting an orphanage, but it could also be talking to a stranger, tipping well and being kind to your server, talking to a coworker about their family trials, or even loving a younger sibling. Holy things are about shining God's light, not your own.

9. When this life is over, your gravestone will not show your social media stats, your résumé, your rejections, or even opinions from your ex-boyfriends. It will have a line, though. This line separates the day you were born with the day you went to heaven. Life is about how you love boldly within that line. Each day is a gift. Use your line to show others love and not to convince them to like you.

10. Some of you may be a bridesmaid twelve times, and some of you may never be a bridesmaid. But pray boldly for your friends. You aren't required to be their favorite, but you are required to love them well.

11. Remember that one friend? The one friend you haven't heard from in a while? Check up on them. Sometimes we get so worried about ourselves, we forget about others. Your legacy is your love, so love others well. Love the people God placed in your life.

12. Appreciate the "God smiles." Look for an opportunity to see God working at the grocery store, the gym, or at work. Don't just be bold with your family or in your career; be bold in the small moments. Look for opportunities and "smiles" from God as He reminds you He sees you.

13. Women were never an afterthought to Jesus. Jesus broke glass ceilings first. Don't let the world tell you otherwise.

14. You can't google wisdom, and no matter how hard you study, you won't find God's will in your textbooks. Wisdom and discernment come from the Holy Spirit. When you don't know how to be bold, remember you know how to pray. That is more than enough.

15. It is really hard to compare yourself to others if you're busy praying for them. Remind yourself they are your teammates, not your competitors. Cheer them on.

16. Your body is more than entertainment for men or peers. Your body is a vessel God can use for His glory.

17. On the day you wonder if your arms are too big or your legs are not muscular enough, I pray you remember your God is enough. You may never be the hottest or the girl with the best body, but thankfully your purpose is about more than being liked.

18. That dream in your heart is there for a reason. If it doesn't work out, you won't lose anything. In fact, even if you fail, you'll have the clarity that comes from knowing you tried.

Do your best, work hard, but never forget God gave you that dream for a reason. And the reason wasn't so you could doubt yourself.

19. You don't have to prove yourself to the middle school bullies from years ago or your family members who doubt you. True boldness comes from knowing who God is, not the insecurity you feel when you try to prove yourself to others.

20. The hurtful words others said to you years ago was sin. Don't let anyone's sin define you. The cross is more powerful than their sin or yours.

21. You can be called to politics or you can be called to art. You can be called to be a wife and you can be called to your job. Focus more on the One who calls you than your calling. Worship God, not your future career or current placement. God can be placing you in positions given by the world for a reason. It might be a job placement, a club exec position, or even being a mother, aunt, or sister. Use these things to glorify Him, not to glorify your own name. Your purpose is first and foremost to know God and love Him.

22. Hagar called God the "God who sees me" (Gen. 16:13). Right now, your God sees you. He sees your insecurities and doubts. He cares for you. He loves you. He led you to this book for a reason. Take time to pray and ask Him to remind you daily that He sees you and He hasn't forgotten about you.

23. Okay, go back to twenty-two again and actually pray this time. I know you probably read on without praying. Never skip over praying.

24. Ten years from now, you'll look back on this season and understand why. You'll see why God removed some people and you'll see the good in some of the goodbyes. There is no such thing as "right person, wrong time." God's timing is always good. Trust that even when you feel hurt, you'll see God's provision. His provision and power are more powerful than your present feelings.

25. The crowd may be loud, but your Savior's love is more powerful. Focus on your Savior.

26. Loneliness is hard. Everyone feels lonely from time to time. Remember even though you feel lonely, you're not alone. You have a God who walks with you and has not left you. You have people in your life who cheer you on, though you may forget about their love. You may feel lonely, but you are not alone.

27. Esther knew her voice was unwanted, but she spoke anyway. As the king's wife, she had to be cleaned with oils to see her husband, and she probably knew better than to give him input on a decree. But she spoke anyway. Maybe you have been silenced before or overpowered by someone else's voice. Speak anyway.

28. Deborah rose to political power and fought the fight God called her to. But it was another woman who got the honor of killing their enemy. Your boldness isn't just for you; it may be leading other women. Pray to be the type of woman who holds the doors for other women and isn't afraid if others walk through the doors you once had to knock at. Real bold women help other women live boldly. Real bold women aren't jealous of others; they live out love and cheer others on.

29. Sarah didn't think God included her in the blessings for her family, so she excluded herself to make it happen for everyone else. Often, the ones excluding us from big things aren't established male CEOs, crazy mothers-in-law, or bullies; it's ourselves. We are the reason we are scared to live boldly. We have believed the lie from the Enemy that God's promises involve others, but not us. Don't try to dilute God's best and make yourself just an afterthought. Trust that God has included you. You are part of His kingdom and of His promise.

30. The woman at the well left her shame at the very place she met Jesus. Yes, you may have a past that makes you want to hide like she did. Yes, you may have people in your hometown who still gossip about you or ex-friends who talk bad about you, but you also have a Savior who says you can leave your shame and the lies you believe about your worth at His feet. Believe this.

31. The woman who touched Jesus' cloak touched only the edge. You may feel like you are barely hanging on to Jesus. Doubt may feel real, and you may be questioning this life and your purpose. Remember, a thread can be enough. Just pray boldly and give God a chance while you hold on to that thread.

32. Mary cared about being a servant for God more than she cared about her body or relationship status. I know you may be struggling with your relationship status or your body image, but God's purpose is bigger than those worldly labels. Do your squats, eat fresh fruit, and go on that coffee date, but remind yourself not to make an idol out of your relationship status or your body.

33. Mary Magdalene went from having seven demons inside her to being one of the first to see the risen Jesus. Don't forget you can go from being the party girl, drained student, overwhelmed mother, wannabe perfectionist, addict, or hot-mess express to being used for big things. Spiritual redemption is important, and I pray you're bold enough to repent and ask your Savior for help. But I also hope that after He saves you, you're bold enough to pick up your cross and follow Him every day. And when you truly follow Jesus, you'll be following the truth and not the opinions of others.

34. Tabitha didn't have much written about her, but she did love well. You and I may never be in a textbook. No one may know our name five thousand years from now. It won't matter if we got that job or proved the mean girl wrong. What would matter is if we loved those around us well, so let's love boldly. Let's do holy things, not main-character things.

35. If you don't have any non-Christian friends, be a little bolder. Find people who need to know the Author of love and show them the love of Jesus. Make friends in the gym, the grocery store, a walking club, or even just next door.

36. Opinions of others will change. There was a girl who didn't like me in college but now messages me how much she misses me. There was also a guy who told me he liked me and then hooked up with someone else. People's opinions about you will change. But God is consistent. He consistently loves you and consistently calls you to do bigger things than be liked.

37. Pray boldly for your friends and your enemies. Don't just pray, "God bless them!" Pray genuinely about their careers, families, health, and more. And you don't even have to tell them you're praying for them; just watch God work.

38. Find peace in the Holy Spirit. You can plan all you want, but life will always have surprises. The world will surprise you, yes, but allow the Spirit to surprise you with peace to endure even the hardest trials.

39. You don't owe everyone trust. You should love everyone and give everyone grace because love and grace come from the cross, but trust comes from wisdom and discernment. Be bold enough to know the difference between your privacy and secrecy. Don't hide your flaws, and always strive to be vulnerable, but what the Holy Spirit tells you to keep private, keep private. It doesn't make you a bad person for needing space to grow; it just makes you human.

40. There will be plenty of people who don't like you, and some who think you and other women are afterthoughts for the gospel. We are called to "go and tell," not to "go and be liked along the way." Live a purposeful life, not a people-pleasing life. One day when your hair is gray and it hurts to get up from the couch, I hope you remember all the moments of adventure that started because you were bold. I hope when you reflect on your younger years, you'll see little moments of courage that led to big God moments. I pray you'll see that God doesn't need perfection; He just needs a yes.

As you close this book, instead of panicking about the emails you need to respond to or worrying about that guy not texting you back, focus on your next yes. Your yes doesn't have to be a career change, even though it could be. Your yes could simply be saying yes to talking to your neighbor or joining a club to meet more nonbelievers. Your yes could be leading a Bible study or running for a local political position. Your yes could be calling a friend you haven't heard from in a while or using your gift of art to paint a mural for a shelter. I hope you do big things, yes, but more importantly I hope your yeses are intentional and bold. I hope you step out of your comfort zone and listen for God's direction.

It is up to you what happens next. Remember these women in the Bible and recognize that God was present then and He is just as present now.

You are not an afterthought. Women are invited to the table and are asked to live this bold life. On the day you wonder, *What will they think?* I hope you will remember these bold women. Instead of asking, *What will they think?* I pray you say, "I am a servant of the Lord. Let Your will be done," like Mary, the mother of Jesus, did. In fact, maybe go write that on a sticky note and place it on your bathroom mirror so you can remember this every day. Let's not miss out on God's purpose. Let's be bold.

CONCLUSION

So What's Next?

I OFTEN WONDER WHERE YOU WILL GO NEXT AFTER YOU finish the book. I truly wish I were sitting with you on the couch, on the beach (if you're lucky enough to be reading this there), or in your dorm room. Maybe you'll go out to eat. Maybe you'll go straight to church and sign up to lead a Bible study. Maybe you'll reluctantly go change a diaper. Maybe you have a final tomorrow and just need to study. Wherever you go, I pray you go boldly.

Fun fact: my freshman year of college I read one of my favorite Christian lifestyle books. Each page was so good. I loved this book and felt intrigued. But want to know what I did after I finished the book? I put on my leather miniskirt and went straight to the bar with friends only to black out. Isn't that sad?

I loved the book, but I didn't think it was true. I didn't think the Christian life was for me. That was for a priest or the perfect good girl, and even though that book told me I was loved, I felt like this role wasn't meant for me.

But here's what I want to remind you: your life is meant for more. There is a warrior in you. There was a warrior in each of these women God found a way to use. So I hope that you're not like me, and when you close this book, you won't go back to your struggle, your insecurity, or your self-doubt. Instead, I hope you'll believe that you are a warrior and that God has a plan for you.

You can do anything boldly so long as you do it for the glory of the Lord. You can leave that toxic relationship, and you can start that business. You can lead a Bible study, and you can get a side hustle so you can save money for your calling. You can start saying no and find rest. You can start a club or invite your coworker to dinner and pray for an opportunity to talk about your faith.

When you choose boldness, it doesn't wait. It won't wait on a better time, and it won't let you believe that lie that you aren't called for big things. Boldness doesn't wait on approval from people whose opinions aren't rooted in Scripture. Boldness doesn't worry about how others will react to you walking in your calling.

Boldness is confident yet humble.

Boldness is daring yet patient.

Boldness is loving yet resilient.

And there is boldness in you that is ready to be lived out today.

We live in a world that tells women a lot of lies. The world tells us to shrink ourselves because we are inferior to men. It also tells us we can do this life on our own. Both are lies. You are not less than, and you can't do this life on your own. If you want to do big and holy things, you need to know and live for your big and holy God.

I'll never forget when a staff member at a church told me, "We want women to take the lead in certain areas one day! We want you to be ready for when that day comes." What's sad is this made me excited! *Change is coming, and women will get cool roles soon*, I thought. I did not realize women could have cool roles now or that in the Bible God gave women cool and purposeful roles.

But then I started paying attention to the women in the Bible. And just like I've shared with you, I saw women in many types of roles who were boldly living out their unique calling. And I wondered, *Why do I have to wait for "one day"? Why can't I walk into this calling today?*

We've heard certain Bible stories multiple times, but many of you may have never heard of Deborah, Tabitha, or Hagar until this book. It saddens me that we as women haven't fully met these bold warriors. But now we know them, and we are better for it. Now the choice is up to you. What are you doing next?

Really, what are you doing next?

I know this question may sound like the one you get at a graduation that you have to respond to with some eloquent answer you're not confident in. But here's what I want to remind you: you don't have to know where you're going to be bold; you just have to know Who you are following.

You have the opportunity to follow the God who sees you and your Savior who loves you. Your boldness comes from who He is and not from your past or personality. We serve a Savior who can use women like you and me to change the world in politics, in our families, with our bodies, with our gifts, and with our stories. You don't have power because of who you are; you have power because of who He is. So boldly walk in your purpose and never forget your God isn't just in heaven wondering where you're going next. He's saying, *Come with Me.* He calls you to Him, walks with you, and makes you bold.

I want to remind you of the two things Mary, the mother of Jesus, said to the angel when she was told she would give birth to the Son of Man. Her first question when she was told she would get pregnant as a virgin was "How will this be?" (Luke 1:34). The angel, though in a much longer way, said, "Because your God is going to do it." And Mary's response to this short, not-that-detailed explanation was "I am the Lord's servant. . . . May your word to me be fulfilled" (v. 38).

You're probably wondering what's next. I am not an angel, but I do want to tell you right now that God's got something cool in store for you. God is going to use you in big ways. It might not be easy, and you may be a little scared at first, but God isn't finished with you yet, and there is a reason and purpose for you. You just need to be bold.

And even though I don't know what is next for you, I pray your response is the same as Mary's: "I am a servant of the Lord. May God's word be fulfilled."

So, here's to going back to changing diapers or checking your email for the fifth time today after you close this book. Here's to maybe going out with an old friend or trying an average restaurant with a new friend. Here's to new adventures, ordinary days, and a God who gives us purpose even in the craziness of life. Your life is meant for big and holy things. You don't need to know the details. You don't need to know how. You just need to know your role, remember these bold women, and choose to live this love. I may not know where you're going next, but I pray you go boldly as you follow the Lord where He leads you.

And the next time you wonder, *What will they think?* I hope you laugh. Your role is not about satisfying others' opinions or convincing them to like you. Who cares what they think? You are living life boldly for the Lord, not living a life to be liked. Focus on loving big more than proving that you're worth loving. He is ready to use you in a big, bold way.

Acknowledgments

IF YOU KNOW ME WELL, THEN YOU KNOW I LOVE SUSHI, I don't know how to fold a T-shirt properly, and the people who surround me have been there with me through it all. Although 2020 was hard for me, I'm thankful that it taught me my purpose. I am thankful I fell in love with God's Word and began to look up to the warrior women in the Bible. But I am also thankful for what 2020 taught me about those I love.

To my dad: I get my humor from you, and I wish I were better at saving money like you. I know my author career doesn't make sense to you, the wise and smart banker, but thank you for always believing in me. Thank you for loving me well.

To my mother: You are kind and gentle. Thank you for loving me well. I am better because of you. I love you big, and I am thankful for your cooking. I may never know how to make your Asian chicken salad, but I pray I learn how to love others like you.

To my grandmother Valentine: I'll never forget that you'd make me banana bread because you knew I didn't like your pound cake, and you'd use your Alexa to tell you the ingredients. Although your eyes aren't what they used to be, you see things with a holy view. I love you. Thank you for having business cards with my name on them and never failing to tell anyone about my career. Thank you for being bold before I knew what bold was. I am stronger because of you.

To my grandmother Herbert: You are kind, and I pray to be as gentle as you. Thank you for loving me, never missing an opportunity to send me a card, and caring for me so well.

To my brother and Ellie: Ellie, thank you for putting up with our crazy family. You are so kind. Thank you for making EJ kinder, and EJ, thank you for caring about me. We are different, yet if there's anyone I know who is bold and good at not caring about what others think, it is you. I remember you warning me in high school that if I wore my Chacos to school people would make fun of me. I then wanted to be like you and wear Chacos to school. I copy you sometimes, but I truly will never be as confident as you. You are a natural leader and I know you'll go far.

To my best friend, Britta: I'm glad you moved to Orlando. I never dreamed of a greater blessing than my best friend moving to my city. We couldn't have written that into our story (and in our predictions each year, we never guessed it), so it had to be God. I love ya big, and I love Owen. Remind him I bought him that Bible book, not you!

To Nora, Lauren, and Dresden: Thank you for a year of reminding me I'm worth it. Thank you for listening to the tears I cried in college and my phone calls still today. I love you guys, and I hope you know you're all stuck with me! Thanks for having front-row seats to my writing career.

To Maile and Ramsey, my amazing roommates: Thank you for loving me well even when I leave my shoes in the living room. I'm thankful for our late-night chats and small house.

To any young girl I discipled or led at camp as a counselor: You are made for big things! Never forget it.

To my agent, Chip, who believed in me so early on: Thank you. I am better because of your advice. Thank you for caring for my career but also caring enough about me to ask in a genuine way how I'm doing.

To Camp Crestridge: Thank you for being the place I found Christ. I truly would not be here without you. I learned about Jesus, my giftings, and what I'm worth at this camp. Thank you for making me better.

To Max and Joe, my trainers at Max Results: Thank you for reminding me that I can always be stronger and pushing me to never give up. I am thankful for our early mornings and what both of you have taught me about working hard.

To my Honda Civic: You are not glamorous, but thank you for reminding me I don't have to be glamorous.

To Beth Moore: Thank you for teaching me that my calling is important. Thank you for opening the doors for many other young women like me to write books. Thank you for being bold. I hope to meet you one day.

To Taylor Swift: Your music has gotten me through all my tough days and been with me through my road trips. You helped me realize the art of storytelling. Thank you for creating the album I listened to at age fifteen and at age twenty-five.

To Fontainebleau High and all my teachers, Johnny V, and the peers I met there who changed me: Thank you for believing in me. A silly selfie at graduation turned into a book deal years later. Life is wild.

To Baylor: I love you forever, Baylor. The school grew me and changed me. Thank you, Baylor, for being Baylor.

To my Bible study friends in Orlando: I love reading God's Word with you all and talking about life. Thank you for being my people.

To the year 2020: You sucked half the time, but you made me better. Thank you for leading me to where I'm supposed to be.

To all the girls reading this who feel stuck, overlooked, and forgotten: I pray you see the boldness inside you and your Savior in front of you. You are worthy, and God wants you. You can run to Him and be honest with Him. He cares for you.

To my faithful God: You have been so kind to me. Thank You for making me bold. I'm sorry for all the times I cared more about being liked than I did about living in Your calling. Thank You for loving me well, and I pray I may be faithful.

About the Author

GRACE VALENTINE IS AN AUTHOR, BLOGGER, PODCAST host, and speaker. Her readers love the fact that she is young, ordinary, and relatable—they say her fresh voice helps them navigate their own faith and lives. Grace's mission is to show others that Christianity is not lame; it is an adventure worth living.

Grace grew up near New Orleans, Louisiana, in a suburban town called Mandeville. She graduated from Baylor University in 2018 with a degree in journalism. She currently resides in Orlando, Florida, where she enjoys going on runs and eating lots of sushi. You can find Grace on Instagram @thegracevalentine, her podcast *Water into Wine*, her Twitter @gracev96, or her website www.gracevalentine.org. Grace loves connecting with her readers, so send her a message!